The Perfection of Wisdom

❖ Wisdom of the East Series ❖

THE BUDDHA IN MEDITATION

[Frontispiece]

The Perfection of Wisdom

The Career of the Predestined Buddhas

A selection of Mahayana Scriptures
translated from the Sanskrit by

E. J. Thomas, M.A., D.Litt.

Charles E. Tuttle Company
Boston • Rutland, Vermont • Tokyo

Published in the United States in 1992 by
Charles E. Tuttle Company, Inc. of
Rutland, Vermont & Tokyo, Japan with editorial offices
at 77 Central Street, Boston, Massachusetts 02109.

Library of Congress Catalog Card Number 91-78172

ISBN 0-8048-1795-2

*This is a facsimile edition of the work originally published
in London by John Murray in 1952.*

PRINTED IN THE UNITED STATES

CONTENTS

EDITORIAL NOTE

WHEN the Wisdom of the East Series first appeared in the early part of this century, it introduced the rich heritage of Eastern thought to Western readers. Spanning time and place from ancient Egypt to Imperial Japan, it carries the words of Buddha, Confucius, Lao Tzu, Muhammad, and other great spiritual leaders. Today, in our time of increased tension between East and West, it is again important to publish these classics of Eastern philosophy, religion, and poetry. In doing so, we hope The Wisdom of the East Series will serve as a bridge of understanding between cultures, and continue to emulate the words of its founding editor, J. L. Cranmer-Byng:

> [I] desire above all things that these books shall be the ambassadors of good-will between East and West, [and] hope that they will contribute to a fuller knowledge of the great cultural heritage of the East.

INTRODUCTION

THE form of Buddhism known as Mahāyāna, the Great Career, has found among Western scholars the same hindrances to its investigation as met them when Pāli Buddhism first came to be known, that is the lack of authoritative texts. When Max Müller in 1883 published the two sūtras of the Happy Land (*Sukhāvatī-vyūha*) he was not able to mention more than seven texts as being " all that we possess of Buddhist Sanskrit literature ", and only six of them belonged to Mahāyāna. The most important of these was the *Lalita-vistara*, which was already known in a French translation from a Tibetan version. It is a life of Buddha from the time when he decided to be born in his last birth down to his enlightenment and first preaching.

The *Lalita-vistara*, " Extended account of the sports " (of the predestined Buddha), is a Mahāyāna sūtra given as the Buddha's own words, and it agrees largely with the story in Pāli accounts of the Buddha's early life. It rests, however, not on traditions of the Pāli form of the legend but on the schools in India, so that there are many variations in detail from the Pāli as well as additional legends.

The discourse begins with the existence of the Bodhisattva (predestined Buddha) in heaven before his last birth. He decides when to be born, in what country, and of what clan and family. He chooses to be born as son of the king of the Sakyas, a people who all belonged to the clan of the Gautamas (Pāli, Gotamas). Hence his usual name, Gautama or Gotama, which is thus a kind of surname. Queen Māyā, who is to be his mother, the wife of king Suddhodana, asks to be allowed to follow for long an austere conduct. She then dreams that a white elephant enters her womb. The brahmins prophesy that she will give birth either to a universal king or a Buddha. The birth in the Lumbinī grove follows, the death of his mother after seven days, the visit of the sage Asita, who prophesies his Buddhahood, the events of his youth, his marriage to Gopā at the age of sixteen, and the three palaces built for him by his father in order to distract him from the thought of renouncing the world. Then the gods remind him of his real purpose. On visiting the park he sees an old man, a sick man, a corpse, and an ascetic. In dread of the ills of this life he makes the Great Renunciation, visits various sages in vain, and then with five disciples practises austerities for six years. At last he finds the right way of meditation, and after elaborate preparations goes to the Bodhi tree. From there the terrific attempts of Māra fail to dislodge him, and he wins enlightenment. He recites the Chain of Causation, and after staying there seven weeks receives food from two passing merchants. Here there is much elaboration of details, but the general course of events is like the Pāli. He doubts whether to preach, but Brahmā comes and persuades him, and he thinks first of going to his old teachers. The gods tell him that they are dead, so he goes to Benares to his five disciples, who had left him when he abandoned his austerities. There he preaches to them the first sermon, *The Turning of the Wheel of the Doctrine*, and converts them.

It may be asked what there is Mahayanist about this sūtra. As summarized here it contains nothing distinctively Mahayanist. The author or compiler was relating events which were the common property of all Buddhists, and he quotes largely from the Scriptures. Yet the Mahayanist character comes out from time to time in several features. Besides the fact that it is expressly called a Mahāyāna sūtra, we find in the introductory words not only the usual disciples assembled to hear the discourse but a large number of Bodhisattvas. The doctrinal aspect of Mahāyāna is not so prominent, but after the account of the first sermon, which is reported in full, we are told that the Bodhisattva Maitreya asks the Lord to expound the Turning of the Wheel to the Bodhisattvas, who have assembled from the ten quarters. He does so in oracular language, saying that the Wheel is profound, without duality, and so on with many other epithets intelligible only to the Bodhisattvas, who are proficient in the doctrine of the Void.

All this belongs to legend. It is not until we come to the reign of Asoka in the 3rd century B.C. that we find Buddhism in connexion with historical events. Asoka became ruler of the greater part of India in 269 B.C., and was crowned four years later. From the latter date, 265 B.C., the Ceylon Chronicles reckon the Nirvāṇa of Buddha as being 218 years before Asoka's coronation, that is, 483 B.C., but there is no evidence that this date was ever recognized outside Ceylon. A more likely date mentioned in several Sarvāstivādin avadānas is that the date of Asoka was not 218 but 100 years after the Nirvāṇa. This is followed by Professor H. Ui and other Japanese scholars, and thus they make the date of the Nirvāṇa not 483 B.C. but 386 B.C.

These chronological questions concern us only in so far as they relate to the question as to the time when Mahāyāna as a school originated. Unfortunately we know nothing of the history of Buddhism between the time of Asoka and the Christian era. The names of a number of schools (traditionally 18) are known, and portions of the Scriptures of some of them have been preserved. The most important of these schools was the Sarvāstivādin, and we now have enough of the Scriptures of this school to know that they were essentially the same as those of the Pāli school in Ceylon. They are arranged in the same four divisions, and the discourses (allowing for the fact that they are in Sanskrit, a language closely related to Pāli) often word for word correspond. But the Sarvāstivādins continued to exist in India for centuries, and they developed a special kind of literature called *avadāna*, 'heroic feat', containing legends of Buddha and his disciples. These contain a doctrine that we do not find in the original Scriptures, that is the teaching that the disciple might aim not merely at becoming an arhat and fully realize the truths taught by the Master, but that he should become a Bodhisattva and aim at winning the supreme enlightenment of a Buddha. Such a disciple does so by passing through many births and accumulating merit until in ten stages he has acquired all the Buddha qualities. In this doctrine there is nothing contradictory to the older teaching. To aim at Buddhahood was exactly the career which the Master himself had chosen, and which future Buddhas would have to undertake. But the doctrine did become a sectarian doctrine when it was taught by the Mahayanists that the career of Bodhisattva should be the career of all.

There was also another school which shows some features of Mahāyāna doctrine, the Mahāsanghika. It had an enormous avadāna, the *Mahāvastu*, 'the great story' of Buddha's career from his last birth to his enlightenment. This work describes ten stages in the Bodhisattva's career, though they are not identical with the Mahāyāna list. It was among these schools in India, not in the Theravāda school of Ceylon, that the Mahāyāna doctrines arose, but it is impossible to give a historical account without historical data. A more profitable beginning will be an examination of Mahāyāna doctrines as we find them expressed in the extant Mahayanist Scriptures.

The two principles of Mahāyāna that specially concern us are the career of the Bodhisattva and the doctrine of the Void. The career of the Disciple as expressed in the first sermon was that he should avoid the extremes of self-indulgence and self-mortification, follow a course of moral training, and meditate on the four Truths until he had fully realized them. This was no selfish goal, for at the same time the monks were exhorted by the Master to go and preach the doctrine, " journeying for the profit of many, for the happiness of many, out of compassion for the world, for the good, profit, and happiness of gods and men ". So the elder Pūrṇa at the risk of his life went to teach the doctrine to some savage border tribes. Upagupta, while still a layman, went and converted Vāsavadattā from her life of sensual indulgence.[1]

To preach the truths to all was also the aim of the Bodhisattva, but while the monk and even the arhat could only teach the Truths that he had learned from the Master, the Bodhisattva aimed at becoming a Buddha, so that if all knowledge of the Truths had perished in the world he could through his Buddha-knowledge realize them again and teach them independently. During all the time that he was training he was heaping up merit, which he could bestow on others. There is no doubt that the career of Bodhisattva was a noble ideal adopted by many who wished for the welfare of their fellow creatures, and it remained so for long. Śāntideva, a Bodhisattva of the 7th century A.D., in his poem [2] thus makes his prayer.

> May I become medicine for the sick and their physician, their support until sickness comes not again.

> May I become an unfailing store for the wretched, and be first to supply them with the manifold things of their need.

---

[1] See the stories of Pūrṇa and Upagupta in *The Quest of Enlightenment*, pp. 40, 44.

[2] *Bodhicaryāvatāra*, translated in this Series as *The Path of Light*.

My own self and my pleasures, all my righteousness, past, present, and future, I sacrifice without regard, in order to achieve the welfare of all beings.

But there was a very different point of view from which the career might be considered by the layman, and it led to a less estimable development.

The Bodhisattva in birth after birth went on accumulating merit in ten stages, until in his last birth but one he had acquired all the qualities of a Buddha. During his career he practised six virtues, the so-called perfections ; almsgiving, morality, patience, heroism, meditation, and wisdom. The term ' perfection ' is ambiguous. What is here meant is not the mere virtue, but a performance by the Bodhisattva of each virtue in its most complete and perfect form, as when prince Vessantara while practising almsgiving gave away all his wealth, the final perfection of wisdom or full knowledge being the gaining of omniscience. The Bodhisattva who had acquired stores of merit, which he wished to bestow on others, became a person to whom laymen could pray. They did so, just as the Hindu laymen round them, who had their tutelary gods, and they were encouraged in this practice by the discourses which were preached to them recounting the beneficent deeds of countless Bodhisattvas. Many of the discourses have no doctrinal significance at all, but consist in the recital of the marvellous achievements of such half-mythical beings.

There is a striking instance of this in the two discourses called *The Sūtra of the Happy Land* (*Sukhāvatī-vyūha*). In the longer sūtra the Buddha tells Ānanda of a disciple named Dharmākara, who on hearing of the achievements of 81 previous Buddhas vowed to become a Buddha and to make a Buddha-field 81 times more excellent. He did so, and became the Buddha called Amitābha " of infinite light ", or Amitāyus " of infinite life ". He now preaches the doctrine in his realm, which is described in great detail as a land of bliss. The smaller sūtra gives a description of this Buddha-field addressed to the elder Sāriputra. Both sūtras teach that any who continue to repeat the name of Amitābha will be reborn in that realm, where they will stay as Bodhisattvas until their career is completed.

These sūtras have given rise to a popular misconception of the doctrine. Every Buddhist who has not attained Nirvāṇa hopes to be born in a happier existence in one of the Buddhist heavens, as may be seen from the stories of the weaver's daughter, who was reborn in the Tusita heaven and of Vāsavadattā, who was reborn among the gods. Amitābha's heaven is only an extension of this doctrine. But a religious feature does appear, which is absent from the courses of training for the monks. This is *bhakti*, devotion. It is devotion to Amitābha, and not any " root of goodness " which ensures being born in the Happy Land. But this birth is only temporary. Those who are born there become Bodhisattvas, and on completing their training they will go to fulfil their mission and finally as Buddhas attain Nirvāṇa. The idea that the Happy Land meant final salvation and a substitute for Nirvāṇa appears to be chiefly due to religionists who could not imagine the Happy Land as being anything else than their own conception of Heaven. Even in Japan the correct view is recognized, for, as Mrs. Suzuki says, " the duration of sojourn in the Pure Land is not eternal, for it is a field for purification and illumination ".[3]

The other chief principle of Mahāyāna is the doctrine of the Void, *śūnyatā*. Every individual thing or entity (*dharma*) is said to be void of reality. Hence in the highest sense things may be said not to exist. This is a truth that is to be meditated on by

[3] *Mahayana Buddhism* (1948), p. 104.

the Bodhisattva in his samādhis, but which is fully realized only when he attains the full enlightenment of a Buddha. It is not surprising that to some early investigators the doctrine appeared to be mere fatuousness and niaiserie, while to others who interpreted voidness as nothingness it was a system of nihilism.

Buddhist thought does not start from such abstractions as matter and mind, but from concrete things called *dharmas*, objects or entities. Such an object might be a living being, a material object, or even a thought. As these entities are compound, they are changing every moment, and nothing can be asserted of them which does not at once become false. What is true of them one moment is not true the next. But it is also the Buddhist doctrine that there is one dharma or thing which is uncompounded. Hence it is unchanging, permanent, immortal. In such words Nirvāṇa, the permanent state, is described. It was also denied that Nirvāṇa at death means the annihilation of the individual. It is the final permanent state of the individual. This conception the Mahayanists developed. It was not only the permanent state of the arhat, but also the permanent reality of everything in its essential existence ; and this reality they called Suchness, *tathatā*, existence as such (*tathā*) without qualification. What it was positively was not stated, as there is nothing in the world of change which can describe it. But Mahāyāna developed schools, which raised new points of view. The older teaching was content to deny reality or independent existence to the changing dharmas, and to seek the one reality by meditation on the one inexpressible suchness. The earliest known commentator, Nāgārjuna (2nd century A.D.), chiefly devoted himself to showing the contradictions in ordinary experience, and hence its unreality. A later school, the Yogāchāras or Vijñānavādins, sought to give a more positive conception of the nature of reality, and called it store-consciousness.

But they retained the two fundamental doctrines of Mahāyāna, the Bodhisattva ideal and the doctrine of the Void. This must be discussed on a later occasion. Other schools that arose made no further contribution to the metaphysical teaching.

MAHĀYĀNA SCRIPTURES

Owing to the lack of accessible texts the relation between Mahāyāna and the older schools has often been misunderstood. The first question for inquirers was naturally to ask what are the peculiar doctrines of Mahāyāna. But this ignores the fundamental question that ought to be put : to what extent are all the schools agreed ? As the *Lalita-vistara* shows, the fundamental doctrines are still there : the Four Truths, the Eightfold Way, and Nirvāṇa as the final goal for all. It has been said that this sūtra contains much Sarvāstivādin material. This is true, but this is just because the material belongs equally to Mahāyāna. The Mahayanists never denied the original doctrines. They had the original discourses, and there is nothing to show that they ever modified the texts. Some commentators speak of the direct and the derived meaning, but this very fact shows that they did not deliberately alter the text itself. They only interpreted it in different ways. Nor did they cut themselves off from other schools. The śrāvakas or disciples of the older doctrine are represented as being present along with the Bodhisattvas at the recital of Mahāyāna sūtras. It was even admitted that the Buddha taught the older doctrine for the sake of those who were not able to grasp the higher teaching.

The Mahāyāna sūtras were first known from Tibetan and Chinese translations, and now many have been found in the original Sanskrit. It will be sufficient to mention here only the most important and those that have been used in the present selection.

The *Lalita-vistara* has been described above. As it is a narrative of events, it contains little doctrinal matter. An important group of discourses is that known as *Prajnāpāramitā*, " the Perfection of Wisdom ". They are of very different length, the longest being of 100,000 verses. Although mainly in prose, they are reckoned by ' verses ', which means 32 syllables of an ordinary stanza. The best known is the *Aṣṭasāhasrikā* in 8,000 verses. The one first known to the west was the *Vajracchedika*, and it unfortunately gave rise to the view that the doctrine of the Void was contradictory nonsense. The *Saddharmapuṇḍarīka*, " the Lotus of the Good Doctrine ", states the career of the Bodhisattva in opposition to that of the disciple, who aims at mere arhatship. Yet it was admitted that the Buddha did teach the disciple's career for the sake of those of little intellect, although finally every other career will be absorbed in the Mahāyāna. The *Daśabhūmika* describes the ten stages of the Bodhisattva's career, and the *Suvarṇaprabhāsa*, " Gold-splendour ", is a loose collection of tales glorifying the Buddhas and extolling its own merits. Other sūtras describe the Bodhisattva's career and his achievements with little reference to doctrine. The *Kāraṇḍavyūha* recounts the marvellous deeds of the popular Bodhisattva Avalokiteśvara. The two *Sukhāvatī-vyūha* sūtras describe the " Happy land ", in which those who enter the Bodhisattva career will stay until they are ready for Buddhahood. *Rāṣṭrapāla-paripṛcchā*, " The question of Rāṣṭrapāla ", deals with the qualities of a Bodhisattva, but the most interesting part is a prophecy of Buddha on the future moral corruptions of the Order, doubtless reflecting the actual conditions of a later time.

NOTE

THE frontispiece shows a figure of Buddha in the attitude of meditation. It is an example of Gandhara art, a form of sculpture which flourished in north-west India in the 2nd century A.D. The execution of these carvings clearly shows Hellenistic influence, but the conception is entirely Buddhistic, and as the many examples of Bodhisattvas show, it is also Mahayanistic. The figure was found in the Swat Valley, and is now in the possession of Pandit C. Jinarājadāsa, President of the Theosophical Society, Adyar, Madras.

I. BUDDHA DECLARES THE NATURE
OF A TATHĀGATA

The Lotus of the Good Doctrine after an elaborate introduction begins with a glorification of the infinite knowledge of a Tathāgata. The disciples present, who belong to the lower career, are astonished. Those who have already attained Nirvāṇa think they have no more to learn, and some out of pride leave the assembly. The term " disciple ", lit. " hearer ", is used throughout of those who are following the lower career. Tathāgata is a frequent epithet of a Buddha, and is used in the same sense. Literally it means " he who has gone thus ", i.e. like former Buddhas, but this sense is not found in the Scriptures, where it is his knowledge of the truth that is emphasized. Another epithet is *Sugata*, " he who has well gone," which is left untranslated.

TATHĀGATAS, Sāriputra, have acquired great skill in devices, knowledge and insight, and the highest perfections. They are endowed with non-attachment, undefeated knowledge and insight, with the (ten) powers of a Buddha, the (four) confidences, the special qualities, the faculties, the powers, the parts of enlightenment, the trances, the releases, the concentrations, the attainments, and the marvellous qualities. The Tathāgatas are proclaimers of various qualities, they have acquired great wonders and marvels. Enough, Sāriputra, let so much be said, Tathāgatas, arhats, perfect Buddhas have acquired the highest marvels. It is only a Tathāgata, Sāriputra, who can teach the things of a Tathāgata that a Tathāgata knows. It is only a Tathāgata who teaches all things, it is only a Tathāgata who knows all things, both what they are, how they are, what they are like, what characteristics they have, and what is their real nature, what, how, what like, of what characteristics and what

13

their real nature is. A Tathāgata sees these things directly and
they are not beyond his sight.

Then the great disciples who were in the assembly led by
Ajnāta Kauṇḍinya, arhats, who had destroyed the corruptions,
twelve hundred who had won the mastery with others who
were following the Disciple's career, monks, nuns, laymen, and
lay women, and those who had set out on the private Buddha's
career, they all thought, " What then is the cause, what is the
reason, that the Lord so excessively extols the skill in devices
of Tathāgatas, by saying ' profound is this doctrine with which
I have been enlightened ', and by saying ' hard is it to be understood by all Disciples and private Buddhas '. Now as only one
release has been declared by the Lord, we also have acquired
the Buddha-qualities on having attained Nirvāṇa, and we do
not understand the meaning of what the Lord has said."

So then the reverend Sāriputra seeing the doubt and perplexity
of the four groups of hearers, and being aware of the delibera-
tions in their minds, and also himself having some doubt about
the doctrine, said at that time to the Lord, " What is the reason,
Lord, what is the occasion, that the Lord so excessively· and
repeatedly extols the skill in devices of Tathāgatas, their knowledge and insight and their teaching of the doctrine, saying again
and again, profound is my doctrine, and hard to understand is
hidden speech. I have never before heard such a discourse on
the doctrine from the Lord, and these four groups of hearers
have fallen into doubt and perplexity. It would be well if the
Lord would explain that with reference to which the Tathāgata
repeatedly utters the praise of the hidden and profound doctrine
of the Tathāgata."

Thereat the Lord said to the reverend Sāriputra, " Enough,
Sāriputra, of telling the meaning. And why ? The world with
its gods will be terrified if the meaning is explained." A second

time the reverend Sāriputra entreated the Lord, " May the Lord tell, may the Sugata tell the meaning. And why ? There are in this assembly many hundreds of beings, many thousands, many hundred thousands, many hundred thousands of crores of millions, who have seen former Buddhas, who are intelligent, and who will believe, admit, and accept what is said by the Lord." (A third time Sāriputra asks.)

So the Lord seeing that the reverend Sāriputra had made his entreaty for the third time said to him, " Seeing that you now entreat the Tathāgata even for the third time, I will give some reply to your entreaty. Therefore, Sāriputra, listen, reflect on it well and deeply. I will tell you."

As soon as this was said by the Lord, then as many as five thousand proud monks, nuns, laymen, and lay women rose from their seats, saluted the Lord's feet with their heads, and left the assembly, so that through their bad root of pride, though they had not acquired, yet imagining that they had acquired, and though they had not attained, imagining that they had attained, and feeling that they had received a wound they left the assembly. And the Lord by his silence consented.

Then the Lord addressed the reverend Sāriputra : " My assembly, Sāriputra, is free from chaff, free from rubbish ; it is established in the essence of faith. Good, Sāriputra, is the departure of those proud ones. Therefore, Sāriputra, I will tell you the meaning."

Lotus, ch. 2.

II. THE ONE PURPOSE OF A TATHĀGATA

Buddha goes on to declare that the omniscience of a Buddha should be the goal for all disciples.   His one purpose is to teach the career that leads to omniscience, and this Great Career, Mahāyāna, is that of the Bodhisattvas, the beings whose aim is *bodhi*, enlightenment.

THE Lord said : at some time and occasion, Sāriputra, a Tathā-gata utters such a teaching of the doctrine as this : just as the flower of an udumbara-fig at some time and occasion appears, even so a Tathāgata at some time and occasion utters such a teaching of the doctrine as this.   Believe me, Sāriputra, I am a truth-speaker.   I am a speaker of what is thus (*tathāvādi*), a speaker of what is not otherwise.   It is hard, Sāriputra, to understand the hidden speech of a Tathāgata.   And why ?   The doctrine has been proclaimed by me with various explanations, expositions, declarations, and interpretations, with hundreds of thousands of different ways of skill in devices.   The good doctrine is to be understood from the Tathāgata as being without logic, beyond the sphere of logic.   And why ?   With one purpose, one thing to do, Sāriputra, a Tathāgata, arhat, perfect Buddha, appears in the world, with one great purpose and one great thing to do.   And what is this one great purpose ?   For the sake and cause of rousing beings to insight into the Tathāgata-knowledge a Tathāgata appears in the world.   It is for the sake and cause of showing them, introducing them, awakening them, bringing them into the Way of the sight of Tathāgata-know-ledge that a Tathāgata appears in the world . . .

Thus, Sāriputra, the Tathāgata performs what is a Tathāgata's one purpose, one thing to do, one great purpose, one great thing to do.   And why ?   Even so, am I a rouser to insight into the

Tathāgata-knowledge. I am a shower, an introducer, an awakener, a bringer into the Way of the sight of the Tathāgata-knowledge. Even so, Sāriputra, in accordance with one career I teach the doctrine to beings, namely, the Buddha-career. There is no second or third career. Everywhere this is the law in the world with its ten directions. And why? The Tathā-gatas, arhats, perfect Buddhas, of the past in the ten directions, in immeasurable, innumerable universes, who have taught the doctrine for the weal and happiness of many, out of compassion for the world, for the good, weal, and happiness of great multi-tudes both of gods and men, all those Lord Buddhas have taught the doctrine to beings in accordance with one career, namely, the Buddha-career, which ends in omniscience, that is, the rousing, showing, introducing, awakening, and bringing of beings into the Way of insight into Tathāgata-knowledge. And those beings who have heard the doctrine from those Tathāgatas, arhats, perfect Buddhas of the past have all attained supreme perfect enlightenment. (The same is repeated for Buddhas in the future and Buddhas in the present.) Thus, Sāriputra, in this way it is to be looked upon, that nowhere in the world with its ten directions is there any indication of a second career much less of a third.

But again, Sāriputra, when Tathāgatas, arhats, perfect Buddhas arise in the decay of a cycle, or with the decay of beings, distress, heresy, life, in such disturbance and decay of cycles, when many are avaricious and with small roots of goodness, then Tathāgatas with their skill in devices teach the one Buddha career as a three-fold career. In that case Disciples, arhats or private Buddhas do not hear of the action of a Tathāgata in bestowing the Buddha career, they do not enter it, nor do they attain enlightenment in it.

Lotus, ch. 2.

III. SĀRIPUTRA'S CONVERSION

In this account of Sāriputra's conversion from following the career of a Disciple to that of a Bodhisattva nothing positive about the lower career is denied. It is even admitted that the Buddha has taught it. This career is enough to rescue beings from the conflagration of worldly existence, but it does not, like the Bodhisattva's career, lead to the ultimate goal of the winning of omniscience.

THE reverend Sāriputra, pleased, delighted, elated, gladdened, and filled with joy, approached the Lord with folded hands, bowed to him, and looking towards him said, " I am filled with wonder and astonishment, Lord, I am filled with excitement at having heard such an utterance from the Lord. And why? Until now I have never heard from the Lord such a doctrine as this, though I have seen other bodhisattvas, and have heard the Buddha-name of bodhisattvas who will be Buddhas in the future, and I am much grieved and pained and dejected by thus not having insight into the sphere of a Tathāgata's knowledge. And when, Lord, I frequently go to lonely mountains, hills, caves, groves, parks, rivers, or the foot of a tree, to meditate in the open air, then I generally abide in this state (thinking that) though entrance into the true nature of things is in name equal, we have been sent out by the Lord on a low career.[1]   And yet at the same time I think that it is our fault and not the fault of the Lord. And why? If we had given heed to the Lord, when he was uttering a lofty teaching of the doctrine, namely about supreme, perfect enlightenment, we should have set out

[1] *Hīnena yānena;* this is one of the few places where Hīnayāna is used in opposition to Mahāyāna. Usually the older teaching is divided into two and spoken of as *śrāvaka-yāna,* disciple's career, and *pratyekabuddha-yāna,* private Buddha's career, the third being the *mahā-yāna.*

18

in those doctrines.   Again, Lord, as at the time when no Bodhi-sattvas were present, we did not understand the hidden speech of the Lord and were in haste, we heard and grasped and learned and meditated and reflected on the first teaching of the doctrine uttered by the Lord.   I pass my days and nights mostly in self-reproach.   Now, Lord, I have reached Nirvāṇa.   Now, Lord, I have attained Nirvāṇa.   Now, Lord, I have become an arhat. Now I am the eldest son of the Lord, the son of his breast, happily born, born from the doctrine, formed from the doctrine, heir of the doctrine, completed by the doctrine.   Now, Lord, I am free from distress, having heard from the Lord such a marvellous utterance as I have never heard before.'

At these words the Lord said to the reverend Sāriputra, " I tell you, Sāriputra, I inform you before the world with its gods, Māra, Brahmā, ascetics and brahmins, that you, Sāriputra, have been ripened by me in the presence of twenty hundred thousand crores of millions of Buddhas for supreme, perfect enlighten-ment, and you have for long been instructed by me.   You have here been furnished in my utterance with the Bodhisattva counsel and the Bodhisattva secret.   You, Sāriputra, do not through the Bodhisattva power remember your preceding vow to practise nor the Bodhisattva counsel and the Bodhisattva secret.   You think you have attained.   I want to bring to your memory the knowledge of your former vow to practise.   I will preach to the disciples this discourse of the doctrine, the *Lotus of the good Doctrine*, a sutrānta of great extent, an exhorta-tion to Bodhisattvas and a possession of all Buddhas.

Further, Sāriputra, in the future, after immeasurable cycles, inconceivable and measureless, after you have learnt the good doctrine from hundreds of thousands of crores of millions of Tathāgatas and have done all kinds of worship to them, and have fulfilled this Bodhisattva course, you shall become a

Tathāgata, Padmaprabha by name, an arhat, a perfect Buddha in the world, endowed with knowledge and conduct, knower of the world, supreme charioteer of men to be tamed, teacher of gods and men, Buddha, Lord." (Further prophecies follow and the applause of the audience.)

So the elder Sāriputra said to the Lord, " My doubt, Lord, is gone, I am free from perplexity on hearing from the mouth of the Lord this prophecy about my supreme, perfect enlightenment. But these twelve hundred who have formerly been set by the Lord on the stage of learners and have been thus admonished and thus instructed, that the doctrine and discipline ends in this, namely, the passing beyond birth, old age, sickness, death and sorrow and the reaching of Nirvāṇa. And these two thousand disciples of the Lord, both those in training and those who have completed it, all those who have shunned the heresy of a self, the heresy of annihilation, all heresies, and who have formed the idea that they are on the stage of Nirvāṇa, they having heard from the Lord this doctrine which is like nothing they have heard before, have fallen into doubt. It would be well if the Lord would speak to these monks in order to dispel their perversity, so that these four groups of the assembly may be free from doubt and uncertainty."

Thereat the Lord said to Sāriputra, have I not told you before, Sāriputra, how the Tathāgata, the arhat, the perfect Buddha, seeing the dispositions of beings, teaches the doctrine to beings of various tendencies and dispositions by means of various applications and expositions, by different explanations of causes and reasons, principles, interpretations, and skill in devices. It is with reference to this supreme, perfect enlightenment that by means of the teaching concerning all things he sets forth the Bodhisattva career. But further, Sāriputra, I will give you a parable to make its meaning still more clear.   *Lotus*, ch. 3.

IV. PARABLE OF THE THREE CHARIOTS

There is only one ultimate goal, and Buddha explains why three careers (*yāna*) are taught. *Yāna* is any means of locomotion, and Burnouf on account of this parable translated it "vehicle"; although in this parable the vehicles are called not *yāna* but *ratha*, "chariots". Apart from metaphors *yāna* is the course any disciple must follow, expressed in the older texts as the Path or Way.

SUPPOSE, Sāriputra, it were like this, that in a certain village or city there is an old man, aged and advanced in years, wealthy, opulent, and with great possessions. He has a large house, high and spacious, which has been long built, and is the abode of two, three, four, or five hundred persons. The house has only one door, and is thatched with straw. The terrace is dropping, the bases of the pillars rotten, and the walls, straw, and plaster loose. Then suddenly the whole house is set on fire on all sides by a great mass of fire. The man has many sons, five, ten, or twenty, and he himself has come out of the house.

Now the man seeing his house blazing with a great mass of fire is afraid, terrified, excited in mind, and he reflects that he is able to get out and escape quickly and safely, unscathed and unburnt by the great mass of fire from his blazing house through the door, but that his sons, young boys, are playing, sporting and diverting themselves with their various toys in the burning house. They do not know or understand or see or think or feel afraid that the house is on fire. Even though scorched by that great mass of fire and touched by that great mass of pain, they do not reflect on the pain, nor does any thought of escaping occur to them.

Now the man is strong and has strong arms, and he reflects,

" I am strong and have strong arms ; what if I were to take all these boys together on my hip and make them escape from the house." Again he reflects, " Now this house has only one entrance. The door is shut, and the boys, being unsteady and fickle and very young, it is to be feared they might ramble about. Through this great mass of fire they might meet with disaster." Thinking that he will warn them he addresses them, " Come, dear boys, come out. The house is burning with a great mass of fire. Do not get burnt here with this great mass of fire and meet with disaster." But the boys do not understand the words of the man who wishes their good. They are not afraid or terrified and do not run away, nor do they understand what the word burning means. On the contrary, they run about here and there, and look again and again at their father. And why ? Because of their ignorance.

So the man reflects that the house is blazing with a great mass of fire, he fears that he himself and his boys through the great mass of fire will meet with disaster, and he thinks of getting the boys to come out of the house through his skill in devices. He knows the dispositions of the boys and understands their inclinations. The boys have many kinds of various delightful, attractive, dear toys of which they are very fond, and which are hard to get. So the man knowing the boys' dispositions says to them, " Those toys of yours, which are so delightful and wonderful, which you grieve for if you don't get, toys of various colours and kinds, such as bullock-chariots, goat-chariots, and deer-chariots, your dear and attractive toys of which you are so fond, I have put them all outside at the door of the house for you to play with. Come, dears, run out of the house. I will give each of you what he would like and what he wants to play with. Come quickly, run out for the sake of the toys." Then the boys hearing the names of those toys so delightful and dear, run quickly out of the burning house, pushing one another with violent haste, saying, " Who will be first, who will be the very first ? " and knocking against one another rush out of the burning house.

So when the man sees that they are safely out, he goes and sits down in the village square in the open air, filled with joy and happiness, free from care and anxiety, and in safety. Then the boys come to their father and say, " Father, give us those different kinds of delightful toys, such as bullock-chariots, goat-chariots, and deer-chariots." So the man gives his boys bullock-chariots, swift as the wind, made of the seven jewels, furnished with seats, hung with strings of bells, lofty, spacious, adorned with marvellous jewels, decorated with jewel-wreaths, adorned with wreaths of flowers, with cotton and woollen rugs, and spread with calico cloth and crimson cushions on each side, and yoked with dazzling white bullocks swift as the wind, led by many men with flying banners. He gives the bullock-chariots swift as the wind, of one colour and one kind, to each of the boys. And why ? Because he is wealthy, and thinks, " Away with giving these boys other vehicles. And why ? They are all my sons dear and beloved. I have great vehicles such as these, and all the boys ought to be thought of equally and not unfairly. I could give such vehicles to all beings, much more to my own sons." At once the boys mount the great vehicles, filled with wonder and amazement.

What do you think, Sāriputra, surely that man has not told a falsehood in having first shown the boys three vehicles, and afterwards having given them great vehicles, splendid vehicles. Sāriputra said, " Certainly not, Lord, certainly not, Sugata. For this very reason the man has not told a falsehood, because through his skill in devices the man has brought them out of the burning house and saved their lives. And why ? It is just through their lives being preserved that they received all the toys. Even if the man had not given the boys a single chariot, yet the man would not have told a falsehood. And why? For the man had at first the idea that he would save the boys from a great mass of pain by some skill in devices. In that way, the man did not tell a falsehood, not to speak of the fact that the man, having the thought that he had abundant treasuries and storehouses, but reflecting on his love for his sons and coaxing them, gave them vehicles of one colour, that is, great vehicles. There was no falsehood, Lord, on the part of the man."

Thereat the Lord said to the reverend Sāriputra : good, good, Sāriputra, so is it, Sāriputra, so is it as you say. Even so the Tathāgata, the arhat, the perfect Buddha is free from all dangers, is wholly, utterly and completely exempt from all misfortunes, despairs, woes, pains, afflictions, and the blindness, darkness, gloom and enveloping obscurations of ignorance ; the Tathāgata is endowed with the Buddha-powers, the confidences, and the special Buddha-qualities ; mighty with the psychic powers he is the father of the world ; he has attained the highest perfection of knowledge of great skill in devices ; he is of great compassion, of unexhausted mind, well-wishing, and sympathetic ; he appears in the threefold world, which with its great mass of pain and affliction is like a house on fire with decayed roof, for the sake of releasing beings who are involved in the pains of birth, old age, and the rest, from passion, hatred, and delusion, for the sake of rousing them to supreme, perfect enlightenment. When he has appeared he beholds beings being burnt, pained, and tortured by birth, old age, and other pains, and on account of their enjoyments and lusts they suffer many kinds of pains. On account of what they are seeking and what they have got in this life they will in the future suffer many kinds of pains in hell, in animal existences, and in the world of the god of Death. They also suffer poverty among gods and men, union with what they dislike, and separation from what they like. Thus passing their lives in this mass of pain they play and sport and divert themselves, they are not afraid or terrified, nor do they know or think or feel startled or desire any escape. There in the threefold world like a house on fire they take their pleasure and run about, and thus involved in this great mass of pain they never form the idea of reflecting about pain.

Then, Sāriputra, the Tathāgata considers thus : " Now I am the father of these beings. I must release them from such a great mass of pain. I must give them the immeasurable, inconceivable happiness of Buddha-knowledge, whereby they may play and sport and divert themselves, and play their games." Then, Sāriputra, the Tathāgata considers thus : although knowing that I have acquired the Buddha-powers, and the psychic powers, if without some device I were to preach to these beings of the Buddha-powers and the confidences of a Tathāgata, they would not leave those things. And why ? These beings are intent on the five pleasures of sense and the delights of the threefold world. They are not released, and they are being burnt, pained and tortured with old age, sickness, death, sorrow, lamentation, pain, misery, and despair. If they are not made to flee from this threefold world like a house on fire, how will they get to know the Buddha-knowledge ?

Thus Sāriputra, like the strong-armed man who without using his strong arms brings the boys out of the burning house by skill in devices, and afterwards gives them great splendid vehicles, so the Tathāgata, though endowed with the Tathāgata powers and the confidences, does not make use of them, but in order to bring beings out of the threefold world, which is like a house on fire, through his knowledge of skill in devices he shows three vehicles, namely, the Disciple's vehicle, the Private Buddha vehicle, and the Bodhisattva vehicle. By means of three vehicles he rouses the longing of those beings, and says, "Do not delight in this threefold world like a house on fire, in these low objects of the senses of sight, hearing, smell, taste, and touch. While you delight in the threefold world you are being burnt and pained and tortured with craving for the five pleasures of sense. Run out of this threefold world, and you will get three vehicles, namely, the Disciple's vehicle, the Private Buddha vehicle, and the Bodhisattva vehicle. On this point I guarantee that I will give you these three vehicles ; get ready to escape from the threefold world " ; and thus I rouse their longing by saying that these are noble vehicles, praised by the noble ones, and full of great delights ; and with these without wretchedness you can play and sport and divert yourselves. In the faculties, the powers, the parts of enlightenment, the trances, releases, concentrations, and attainments you will experience great delight, and will be full of great joy and happiness.

Then, Sāriputra, those beings who are naturally wise put their full faith in the Tathāgata, the father of the world. And having full faith they apply themselves to the Tathāgata's teaching and exercise themselves in it. Some beings there are who, desiring to follow what they hear from the voice of another, apply themselves to the Tathāgata's teaching to win enlightenment into the four noble Truths for the sake of attaining their own Nirvāṇa. These are called those who desiring the Disciple's vehicle flee from the threefold world like the boys who flee from the burning house desiring deer-chariots. Others desiring the knowledge of self-control and tranquillity without a teacher apply themselves to the Tathāgata's teaching to win enlighten-ment by means of causes and conditions for the sake of attaining their own Nirvāṇa. These are called those who desire the

Private Buddha vehicle, who flee from the threefold world like the boys who flee from the burning house desiring goat-chariots. Still others desiring the knowledge of the Omniscient, the Buddha knowledge, the knowledge of the Self-existent, knowledge without a teacher, apply themselves to the Tathāgata's teaching, to win the enlightenment of the Tathāgata's powers, and confidences, and happiness of many, out of compassion for the world, for the sake of great multitudes, for the welfare and happiness of gods and men, for the sake of attaining the Nirvāṇa of all beings. These are called those who desiring the Great Vehicle flee from the threefold world. For this reason they are called Bodhisattvas, Great Beings. They are like the boys who flee from the burning house desiring bullock-chariots.

And just as that man, when he sees that the boys have fled from the burning house and have escaped from danger into calm and safety, seeing that he has great wealth gives the boys each one splendid vehicle, even so, Sāriputra, the Tathāgata too, when he sees many millions of beings released from the threefold world, who are released from pain, danger, fear, and trouble, who have been made to flee through the Tathāgata's teaching, who are released from all dangers, troubles, and wildernesses, and brought to the bliss of calm. Then at that time, Sāriputra, the Tathāgata considers that he is in possession of his great treasury of Buddha-powers, and confidences, and knowing that they are all his sons, brings those beings to the attainment of Nirvāṇa by means of the Buddha-vehicle. He does not speak of any being attaining individual Nirvāṇa. He causes all those beings to attain Nirvāṇa through attaining the Nirvāṇa of a Tathāgata, the great Nirvāṇa. And those beings who are released from the threefold world, to them the Tathāgata gives the noble trances, releases, concentrations, and attainments of supreme happiness as delightful toys, all of the same colour. Just as the man did not speak falsely when after showing the boys three vehicles he gave them each one great vehicle adorned with the seven jewels, decked with all adornments, of one colour, one splendid vehicle, one supreme vehicle, even so the Tathāgata does not speak falsely when at first through his skill in devices he shows three different vehicles and afterwards causes beings to attain Nirvāṇa through the Great Vehicle. And why ? The Tathāgata possesses abundant treasuries and storehouses of his Buddha-powers, and confidences, and is able to set forth to all beings the doctrine of the knowledge of the Omniscient. Even in this way, Sāriputra, is it to be considered, that the Tathāgata by the use of his knowledge of skill in devices thus teaches the Great Vehicle.

Lotus, ch. 3.

V. THE PRODIGAL SON

The conversion of Sāriputra is followed by the conversion of other disciples, who on discovering that their true goal is not merely Nirvāṇa but the winning of omniscience explain it by a parable.

Now the elders Subhūti, Mahākātyāyana, Mahākāśyapa, and Mahāmaudgalyāyana on hearing this doctrine never heard before, and the prophecy from the Lord about Sāriputra that he would become a supreme, perfect Buddha, were filled with astonishment and amazement, and rose from their seats, approached the Lord, arranged their upper robes on one shoulder, and placing their right knees on the ground, folded their hands, looked at the Lord, bowed their bodies, and said : We, Lord, are old, aged, and advanced in years. We have grown old as elders in this assembly of monks and have reached Nirvāṇa. So we have been prevented from reaching supreme perfect enlightenment, we are unable and incapable of exerting effort . . . But now having heard from the Lord the prophecy of supreme, perfect enlightenment even for disciples, we are amazed and astonished and have received great gain. Today we have suddenly heard such an utterance of the Tathāgata as never before. We have received a great jewel, a priceless jewel, an unsought, unlonged-for, unimagined, unwished-for great jewel have we received. A thought occurs to us, Lord, a thought occurs to us, Sugata.

Just as if, Lord, a certain man were to depart from his father's presence and go to another country. He remains there many years, twenty, thirty, forty, or fifty years. The man grows up and is poor. In search of a living he goes for food and clothing, he goes through the ten quarters and reaches another country.

His father has also gone to a certain country and has become wealthy with stores of corn and gold, possessing gold and silver, gems, and pearls, with many slaves, workmen, and servants, with many elephants, horses, chariots, oxen, and sheep. He has a great retinue, he is wealthy in great countries due to business, farming, and trade.

Then the poor man in search of food and clothing roams through villages, cities, towns, countries, kingdoms, and capitals, and comes to the city where the rich man his father dwells. So his father always thinks of his son whom he has lost for fifty years. He thinks, I am old, I have great wealth, and I have no son. May I not die and all this be lost without being enjoyed. He thinks again and again of his son. Alas, I should die in peace if my son could enjoy this wealth.

So the poor man in search of food and clothing in time reaches the house of his wealthy father. His father is at the door of his house attended by a great retinue of brahmins, warriors, and men of the trading and servile castes, seated on a great seat with a footstool adorned with gold and silver, doing business with gold and silver in hundreds of thousands . . . The poor man thinking he must be a king or a royal minister, and that there is nothing for him there, goes off to a poor street, where he can get food and clothing with little trouble. But his father sees him and remembers him, and sends swift messengers after him. They lay hold of him, and he is terrified. But though he declares that he has committed no fault they carry him off. He faints, and the messengers take him to his father, who says, " Do not bring him here, sprinkle him with cold water, and say no more to him." And why ? He knows that the poor man is of low intentions but of high ability, and that he is his son.

So the householder through his skill in means tells no one that the poor man is his son. He tells one of his men to go to

him and say, " Go wherever you like, you are free." The poor
man amazed goes to the poor street for food and clothes. The
householder in order to get him back uses skill in means. He
sends two dark, weak men to offer to his son twice as much
daily, if he will come and work in the householder's house.
If he asks what he is to do, they are to say, " You are to clean
up the sweepings with us two." The two men and the poor
man then get their wages by sweeping up in the house of the
wealthy man, and they live on the premises in a corner on
straw. He looks through a window at his own son cleaning
up the sweepings and is amazed.

He comes down from his house, removes his ornaments, goes
to him and promises him better work and higher pay . . .
" Look on me as your father. And why ? I am old and you
are young. You have done much work for me in sweeping,
and I have never seen any dishonesty or crookedness in you.
Be from this day like my own son."

So the householder calls the poor man ' son ', and the poor
man looks upon the householder as his father. In this way the
householder through love and longing for his son makes him
clean up the sweepings for twenty years. Then at the end of
twenty years the man is entrusted with the house ; he can go
in and out, and he still lives in a corner on straw.

Then the householder becomes ill and considers that the time
of his death is near. He says to the man, " Come, sir, this is
my abundant store of gold and treasures. I am sick and wish
for someone to whom I may give them, who will take them
and store them up. Take possession of all. And why ? As
I am master of this property, so be you master, and let nothing
of it be lost."

So the man takes charge of the wealth, but has no wish for
it himself, not even as much as a measure of barley-flour, and

he still lives in a corner on straw reflecting on his state as a poor man.

Then the householder seeing that the man is able and watchful, that his mind is ripened and softened, and that through his former guardianship he has passed beyond the thought of his poverty and is ashamed of it and loathes it, when his death draws near he brings the poor man and a large number of his relatives before the king or a royal minister and in the presence of town and country people makes an announcement : Listen, sirs, this is my true son, begotten by me. Fifty years ago he disappeared from a certain city. His name is so-and-so, and I am so-and-so by name. From that city I came here seeking him. He is my son, I am his father. All that is my property I hand over to this man, and all the wealth that is mine he knows as his. So at that time the poor man hearing such a proclamation is amazed, and thus reflects : now all at once I receive this gold and treasures.

Even so, Lord, we are the sons, the image of the Tathāgata, and the Tathāgata, like the householder, says to us, " You are my sons." And we, Lord, are oppressed by the three painful-nesses. What are the three ? The painfulness of pain, the painfulness of compounds, the painfulness of change, and we have low dispositions in transmigration. Hence we have been caused by the Lord to think of many base things like sweepings. It is these on which we are intent and busied and eager, and we are desiring and seeking merely Nirvāṇa as our day's wages. We are delighted with getting that Nirvāṇa. We think we have received much by being intent and busy and eager on those things that we have got from the Tathāgata. The Tathā-gata understands the lowness of our dispositions ; hence the Lord reflects upon us, he does not communicate with us or declare that this Tathāgata's treasury of knowledge shall be ours. The Lord through his skill in means establishes us as heirs to this treasury of Tathāgata-knowledge. We have no wish for it, Lord, for we understand that this is serviceable to us, namely, to receive Nirvāṇa like daily wages. We, Lord, make a noble exposition of the doctrine concerning the Tathā-gata-knowledge and insight of Bodhisattvas, great beings. We explain, show, and demonstrate the Tathāgata-knowledge, though we do not wish for it. And why? The Tathāgata through his skill in means comprehends our dispositions, and that we neither know nor understand, namely, that which has now been spoken by the Lord, how we have become the sons of the Lord, and the Lord causes us to remember that we are heirs of the Tathāgata-knowledge. And why? For we have become sons of the Tathāgata. We have gained the jewel of omniscience.

Lotus, ch. 4.

VI. THE SEARCH OF THE BODHISATTVA
EVER-WEEPING

The story of Ever-weeping (Sadāprarudita) forms the conclusion of *The Perfection of Wisdom in 8000 verses*. It not only gives an idea of the aspirations of a Bodhisattva, his longing to bring welfare to all beings, but it also affords some explanation of the doctrine of the Void, as will be seen in a later chapter.

AGAIN, Subhūti, the Perfection of Wisdom should be sought as it was sought by the Bodhisattva, the Great Being, Ever-weeping, who is now practising the religious life in the presence of the Tathāgata Bhīshmagarjitanirghoshasvara.

Thereat the elder Subhūti said to the Lord : How, Lord, did Ever-weeping search for the Perfection of Wisdom ? The Lord said : Ever-weeping, Subhūti, formerly sought the Perfection of Wisdom without caring for his body, indifferent about his life, and independent of gain, honour, and praise. While he was searching and had gone to the forest, he heard a voice from the sky : Go, noble youth, in the eastern direction, and there you shall hear the Perfection of Wisdom, and so go that you let no reflexion arise about weariness of body, no reflexion about sloth and torpor, food, drink, night and day, cold or heat. Make no application of your mind internally or externally, and do not go looking to the left or the right, or to the south, east, west, north, the zenith, the nadir, or the inter-mediate quarters. So go, noble youth, that you do not waver about (the heresies of) a self, individuality, about body, sensa-tion, perception, the mental aggregates, and consciousness ; for he who wavers therein is unstable, and much more is he unstable about the things of the Buddha. He who is unstable about the things of the Buddha wanders in transmigration. He who wanders in transmigration does not wander in the Perfection of Wisdom. He does not attain the Perfection of Wisdom.

Thereat Ever-weeping said to the voice : even so will I do, and why ? Because I wish to bring light to all beings, I wish to bring them the things of the Buddha. So the voice said to Ever-weeping : good, good, noble youth, Ever-weeping. Now Ever-weeping again listened to the voice, and thus he heard : It is by producing the conviction, noble youth, that all things are void, signless, and undetermined that you must search for the Perfection of Wisdom, and you must meditate by shunning a sign, real being, and the view that there are beings. You must shun bad friends, and you must cultivate good friends and be devoted to them and serve them, and also those who teach the doctrine that all things are void, signless, unarisen, unborn, unceased, and without real existence.

Thus as you advance, noble youth, in no long time you will hear the Perfection of Wisdom, either from a book or from the person of a monk who recites the doctrine. And from whom you hear the Perfection of Wisdom you must cause the idea of a teacher to arise, and you must practise it with thanks and gratitude, thinking, this is my good friend, from whom I am hearing the Perfection of Wisdom, and hearing which I shall quickly reach the stage of not turning back and draw near to supreme, perfect enlightenment. I shall be born in Buddha-fields not deprived of Tathāgatas, arhats, perfect Buddhas. I shall avoid the unlucky times, and shall enjoy the times of good fortune . . .

Now when the Bodhisattva Ever-weeping had got this instruction from the voice he journeyed towards the eastern quarter, and before he had gone far he thought, I did not ask the voice how far I ought to go. So he stood on a plot of ground and weeping, lamenting, grieving, and sorrowing he thus thought, in this spot I will stay for one, two, three, four, five, six or seven days and nights, and I will let no reflexion rise about weariness of body, sloth and torpor, food, drink, day and night, cold or heat, as long as I do not hear the Perfection of Wisdom.

Just as when a man whose only son has died is filled with great grief, through sorrow for his son, and no other reflexion arises than reflexion to his son, even so in the Bodhisattva Ever-weeping at that time no other reflexion arose than this, when shall I hear the Perfection of Wisdom ?

So then, as Ever-weeping was there thus distressed, the form of a Tathāgata stood before him and gave a sign of approval : good, good is it, noble youth, that you utter this speech. For even so has the Perfection of Wisdom been sought by previous Tathāgatas, arhats, perfect Buddhas, who had formerly followed the Bodhisattva career, as you are now searching. Therefore, noble youth, with this heroism, this perseverance, this wish, this will, go to the eastern quarter. There 500 leagues away is a city named Gandhavatī, built of the seven jewels, surrounded by seven walls, seven moats, and seven rows of palm trees. It is twelve leagues in length and twelve in breadth, prosperous, wealthy, peaceful, with abundant food, and with a great popula-tion. (An elaborate description follows of the city and of the house of Dharmodgata, the Bodhisattva, who is to teach Ever-weeping.)

In the middle of the cross-roads of the city the inhabitants prepare a seat for Dharmodgata the Bodhisattva. There he sits down and teaches the Perfection of Wisdom . . . And there many hundreds of beings, many thousands, many hundreds of thousands of gods and men are assembled and listen. Go, noble youth, into the presence of Dharmodgata the Bodhisattva.

From him you will hear the Perfection of Wisdom. For he for long will be your good friend, a shower, a rouser, an exciter, a thriller for winning supreme, perfect enlightenment . . .

Now the Bodhisattva Ever-weeping on hearing this was delighted, elated, enraptured, gladdened, and filled with joy and happiness . . . And standing in that place he heard the Bodhisattva Dharmodgata teaching the Perfection of Wisdom. And as he listened the idea of the independence of all things arose, and many ways of entering into samādhi (concentration) came before him. (Here follows a list of over sixty samādhis, each expressing different aspects of meditation on the Void.)

Abiding in these samādhis he saw the Buddhas in the ten quarters, immeasurable and innumerable, preaching the Perfection of Wisdom to Bodhisattvas. And the Tathāgatas gave a sign of approval and showed him encouragement. They said : even so, noble youth, the Perfection of Wisdom was sought by us formerly, when following the Bodhisattva course, and as we sought, just these samādhis were obtained as you have now obtained them, and having obtained them and gone on our course we were established in the Perfection of Wisdom . . . You must arouse deep reverence for good friends, and show love and good will, since Bodhisattvas who have won good friends are quickly enlightened with supreme, perfect enlightenment.

So Ever-weeping said to those Tathāgatas, who is my good friend ?

They said to him : for a long time, noble youth, you have been implored by Dharmodgata for supreme, perfect enlightenment, and controlled through skill in devices of the Perfection of Wisdom in the things of the Buddha. He is your controller and good friend, and should be kept in mind with gratitude, recognition, and honour . . .

So the Tathāgatas after consoling the Bodhisattva Ever-weep-

ing disappeared, and the noble youth arose from those samādhis.
And after rising he thought, whence have those Tathāgatas
come and where have they gone ? Not seeing the Tathāgatas
he fell into great distress and pain. He thought, the noble
Dharmodgata the Bodhisattva has acquired the spells, attained
the five higher knowledges : he has performed his office under
former Buddhas, he has been my controller and good friend,
and for long has wrought my good. What if I go and approach
Dharmodgata about this, and ask him whence the Tathāgatas
have come and where they have gone. (Ever-weeping has a
series of adventures before he is finally able to put his question
to Dharmodgata.)

Aṣṭasāhasrikā, ch. 30.

VII. THE QUESTION OF EVER-WEEPING

Ever-weeping puts his question to Dharmodgata by first recounting how he began his search. He tells how he was instructed by Tathāgatas to go to a city where he would find a Bodhisattva preaching the Perfection of Wisdom, and how after having done so and having practised many forms of meditation other Tathāgatas came to encourage him and then disappeared. Where, asks Ever-weeping, did those Tathāgatas come from, and where did they go?

Dharmodgata's reply furnishes one of the clearest statements in the sūtras of the doctrine of the Void. It starts from the same principle as that which faced the earlier Buddhists, whether a released person can be said to exist after death.[1] As such a being is freed from everything belonging to the world of sense, there is nothing by which he can be described. His existence in any terms that apply to the world of sense is indescribable. This principle is here applied to all individual things, and they are called void. But the result is not nihilism, for behind everything phenomenal is the ultimately real, the summit of reality, Suchness, existence as such, without any qualification. The Tathāgatas are Suchness, the only reality.

I ASK you (says Ever-weeping speaking of the Tathāgatas who had appeared to him) whence did those Tathāgatas come, and where have they gone? Teach me, noble youth, the coming and the going of those Tathāgatas, so that we may know the coming and going of those Tathāgatas. May we not be deprived of the sight of those Tathāgatas.

Thereat the Bodhisattva Dharmodgata said to Ever-weeping: the Tathāgatas, noble youth, come from nowhere nor do they go. For Suchness is unmoving, and that which is Suchness is the Tathāgata. For non-arising does not come or go, and that

[1] See *The Road to Nirvāṇa*, pp. 62, 70.

which is non-arising is the Tathāgata. For no coming or going of the summit of reality is known, and that which is the summit of reality is the Tathāgata. For no coming or going of the Void is known, and that which is void is that Tathāgata. For no coming or going of fitness is known, and that which is fitness is the Tathāgata. For no coming or going of absence of passion is known, and that which is absence of passion is the Tathāgata. For no coming or going of cessation is known, and that which is cessation is the Tathāgata. For no coming or going of the element of space is known, and that which is the element of space is the Tathāgata. For the Tathāgata is not from other things, and that which is the Suchness of these things, and that which is the Suchness of all things, and that which is the Suchness of the Tathāgata is this one Suchness. There is no duality of Suchness. This one Suchness is Suchness. Suchness in counting is not reckoned as two or three because of its non-reality. Just as a man heated in the hot season, in the last of the hot months, at midday might see water flowing in a mirage, he would run to it, thinking, there will I drink water, there shall I find something to drink. What do you think? Do you think whence the water is coming or where it goes, to the east to the great ocean, or to the south or the west or the north? Ever-weeping said, the water in the mirage does not exist, much less is its coming or going known, and the man heated by the hot season, being naturally ignorant and stupid on seeing the mirage, forms the idea of water where there is no water. Besides, water does not exist there in reality.

Dharmodgata said, even so, noble youth, even so. Even so do those who are intent on the sight or sound of a Tathāgata imagine that a Tathāgata comes and goes. And those who imagine that a Tathāgata comes and goes must all be called ignorant and stupid, just like a man who forms the idea of water where there is no water. And why? Because a Tathāgata is not to be seen through his material body (*rūpakāya*). Tathāgatas are essential bodies (*dharmakāya*), and the real nature of things (*dharmatā*) does not come and go. Just so there is no coming and going of Tathāgatas. Just as in the case of an elephant formed by means of magic or a horse or chariot or foot-soldier, there is no coming or going, so there is no coming or going of Tathāgatas. Just as a man who has gone to sleep might dream that he sees one Tathāgata, or two, three, four, five, six, seven, eight, nine, ten, twenty, thirty, forty, fifty, a hundred, a thousand or still more. On waking up he would not see even one. Now what do you think, whence have the Tathāgatas come or where have they gone? Ever-weeping said, in the dream no manifestation of any thing was known, for the dream spoke falsely.

Dharmodgata said, even so all things have been said by the Lord to be like a dream. They who do not duly know that all things have been expounded by the Tathāgata as being like a dream, persist in viewing a Tathāgata through his body as name or as form and imagine that Tathāgatas come and go. So through not knowing the real nature of things those who imagine that Tathāgatas come and go are ignorant and common people, they have all gone to transmigration with its six destinies or are going or will go. They are all far from the Perfection of Wisdom, they are all far from the things of a Buddha.

Now they who say that all things are like a dream, rightly know that it has been taught by the Tathāgata that all things are dreamlike. They do not imagine anything as coming or going, as arising or ceasing. And they who do not imagine the coming or going of anything, nor arising nor cessation, know the Tathāgata through the real nature of things, and do not imagine that Tathāgatas come and go.   And they who know that the true nature of things is like the Tathāgata are in their course near to supreme, perfect enlightenment, and they are following their course in the Perfection of Wisdom.

Aṣṭasāhasrikā, ch. 31.

VIII. THE BUDDHA'S LENGTH OF LIFE

The question of the absolutely real or Suchness is discussed in the *Lotus* from a different point of view from that of Ever-weeping. Maitreya asks the Buddha how he can have taught such an enormous number of beings in the space of forty years. The Lord explains that his life did not begin with his birth among the Sakyas. He has existed for ages, but for the sake of converting beings he makes the appearance of being born in the world. In the same way the real world does not pass away. The world of Suchness is without change, for it is only the world that appears to the senses that is void. This leads to the further conclusion that the reality of Nirvāṇa, of Buddha, and of Suchness are the same.   This was expressed by a Later school in the doctrine of the three Bodies of Buddha, his apparitional body by which he is born in the world of sense, his body of bliss, in which he now preaches to Bodhisattvas in one of the heavens, and his body of absolute reality, the *dharma-kāya*. Only the last is real in the highest sense.

Now the Lord addressed the whole troop of Bodhisattvas : "Trust in me, noble youths, and believe in the Tathāgata who speaks the truth." A second time and a third time he thus addressed them. So the whole troop of Bodhisattvas with Maitreya at the head folded their hands and said to the Lord, "May the Lord speak on this matter, may the Sugata speak ; we will believe what the Tathāgata says." A second time and a third time they spoke thus.

So the Lord for the third time perceiving the entreaty of those Bodhisattvas addressed them : then listen, noble youths. Such is the force and power in my possession that this world with its gods, men, and asuras thinks that formerly the Lord Sakyamuni, the Tathāgata, renounced the world, going out from a Sakya family, and at the great city of Gayā went to the excellent

Bodhi-tree, and was enlightened with supreme, perfect enlightenment. Not thus should it be considered, but rather that many hundreds of thousands of crores of millions of cycles ago was I enlightened with supreme, perfect enlightenment.

Since the time, noble sons, when in this Sahā universe I have taught the doctrine to beings and in other hundreds of thousands of crores of millions of universes, and the intermediate Tathāgatas, arhats, perfect Buddhas beginning with Dīpankara have been praised by me for the sake of their attaining Nirvāna, these things have been produced by me through my method of teaching the doctrine with skill in devices.

And further, noble youths, the Tathāgata considering the various states of knowledge of the faculties in beings who arise from time to time, and the extent of applying their strength, declares his name, and in each case declares his attaining of Nirvāna, and so in each case gives delight to beings by various kinds of doctrinal discourses. In that case, noble youths, the Tathāgata speaks to beings of various dispositions whose roots of goodness are few, and who have many depravities, and says thus : "I am young, monks, I have renounced my family, and have lately become enlightened with supreme, perfect enlightenment." But again, noble youths, when the Tathāgata having thus long ago attained enlightenment speaks thus, saying, "I have lately attained enlightenment," it is for no other reason than to ripen beings and to take them across that these discourses of the doctrine have been spoken, and all these discourses have been spoken by the Tathāgata for the sake of disciplining beings.

And the speech which the Tathāgata utters for disciplining beings either by showing himself or by his own authority or by the authority of another, whatever the Tathāgata declares, all those discourses of the doctrine spoken by the Tathāgata are true, and there is no false speech of the Tathāgata in them.   And why ?   Because the threefold world is seen by the Tathāgata as it really is.   It is not born, it dies not, it passes not away, it arises not, it transmigrates not, it attains not Nirvāṇa.   It is not real, not unreal, not existent, not non-existent, not false, not unfalse, not otherwise, not thus.   The threefold world is seen by the Tathāgata not as ignorant, common men see it.   The Tathāgata has the nature of seeing things directly.   Surely in that case he has the nature of being without confusion.   Herein whatever speech the Tathāgata declares is all true, not false, not otherwise.

And further, to beings with various modes of life, various pursuits, who act with various ideas and fancies, for the sake of producing in them the roots of goodness, he declares to them different discourses of the doctrine with different principles. For what has to be done by the Tathāgata that the Tathāgata does.   Having long ago attained enlightenment the Tathāgata ever stays with unlimited length of life.   The Tathāgata without having attained Nirvāṇa makes a show of attaining Nirvāṇa for the sake of those who have to be trained.   And not even today, noble youths, is my ancient course as Bodhisattva completed, nor is the length of my life fulfilled.   But again, even today twice as many hundreds of thousands of crores of millions of cycles will be required for completing my length of life.   Again, noble youths, though not attaining Nirvāṇa, I now announce my attaining of Nirvāṇa.   And why ?   In this way I ripen beings, lest if I were to stay for a very long time, and through being often seen, beings in whom the roots of goodness have not been formed, beings deprived of merit, wretched, eager for lusts, blind, wrapped in the net of false views, if they saw that the Tathāgata stays, would get the idea that it is mere sport, and would not form the idea that a Tathāgata is hard to obtain, (thinking) we are near to the Tathāgata. They would not exercise energy to escape from the threefold world, and would not form the idea that a Tathāgata is hard to obtain. Hence, noble youths, the Tathāgata through his skill in devices has declared to those beings, " Hard to obtain, O monks, is the appearing of a Tathāgata." And why? Because during many hundreds of thousands of crores of millions of cycles those beings may have the sight of a Tathāgata or not. Hence, noble youths, making use of that principle I say thus, " Hard to obtain, O monks, are the appearings of Tathāgatas." When still more they see that the appearings of Tathāgatas are hard to obtain, they will be filled with the thought of amazement and grief, and when they do not see Tathāgatas, arhats, perfect Buddhas, they will have a longing to see them. Their good roots produced by reflecting on the principles of a Tathāgata will for long be to their profit, good, and happiness. Considering this matter the Tathāgata, though he does not attain Nirvāṇa, announces his attaining of Nirvāṇa for the sake of training beings.

Lotus, ch. 15.

IX. THE BODHISATTVA'S FIRST STAGE

The *Daśabhūmika* is the discourse on the ten stages of a Bodhisattva. When he has completed them he acquires all the qualities of a Buddha, and has only to be born once more and then become a Buddha, preach, and attain Nirvāṇa. First the thought of enlightenment arises, and he makes the vow to attain omniscience. In the discourse the vow is expanded by stating the different actions required, such as going to worship Buddhas, going to see all the earthly acts of Buddhas, ripening beings, and finally performing all the acts of a Buddha.

WHEN the Bodhisattvas have well accumulated the roots of goodness, have well lived their lives, have well borne their burdens, have well attended on the appearings of Buddhas, have well amassed good qualities, have well attached themselves to good friends, have acquired good motives and abundant intentions, are endowed with high dispositions, and tend to pity and compassion, the thought of enlightenment arises.

For their desire for Buddha-knowledge, for attaining the (ten) powers of a Buddha, for attaining the (four) great confidences, for acquiring the Buddha-qualities of sameness, for saving all the world, for the purification of great pity and compassion, for attaining complete knowledge in the ten directions, for purifying without attachment all Buddha-fields, for perceiving the one moment (of the appearance of a Buddha) in the three times (past, present, future), and for great confidence in turning the Wheel of the doctrine, the thought of enlightenment arises in Bodhisattvas.

A Bodhisattva through the sudden arising of the thought passes over and goes beyond the stage of the common man. He becomes born to the Bodhisattva-rule, he becomes irreproachable in the family of the Tathāgatas, he is removed from all discussion about birth, he goes beyond all destinies of the world, he abides in a supramundane destiny, he is well established in the real nature of Bodhisattvas, through the nearness of Bodhisattvas he is attached to sameness, he is bound to the lineage of the Tathāgatas of the three times (past, present, and future), and his final aim is enlightenment. Furnished with such qualities as Bodhisattva he is established on the stage of Joyous (*pramudita*) with the application of steadfastness.

The Bodhisattva now standing on the Joyful Bodhisattva stage abounds in joy, graciousness, delight, elation, elevation, eagerness, energy, with freedom from rage, from wish to injure, and anger. Thus the Bodhisattva becomes joyful, remembering the Lord Buddhas, the Buddha qualities, the Bodhisattvas, the Bodhisattva practices, the purification of the Perfections, the distinctions of the Bodhisattva stages, their dispersal, the exhortation and instruction of Tathāgatas, the achieving of the good of beings. He becomes joyful remembering his purpose to enter into the knowledge of all the Tathāgatas, and becomes still more full of joy.

Saying, I am separated from the sphere of the whole world, I have passed over to nearness to the Buddha stage, I have gone far from the stage of the ignorant and common man, I am near to the stage of knowledge, I am cut off from falling into any evil destinies, I have become a support for all beings, I have drawn near to beholding all the Tathāgatas, I have arisen in the sphere of all the Buddhas, I have attained to the sameness of all the Bodhisattvas. Gone are all my fears and terrors and stupefactions. So saying he displays joy. Why is that? Because as soon as a Bodhisattva reaches the stage of Joyous four fears entirely disappear, namely, the fear about getting a livelihood, the fear of disgrace, the fear of an evil destiny, and the fear about confidence in assemblies. Why so? Because with the disappearance of the idea of self he has no affection for self, much less for anything subordinate. Hence he has no fear about a livelihood. Nor does he long for any honour through contact with anyone, except for the thought that he must apply every kind of help to these beings. Hence he has no fear of disgrace. With the disappearance of the view of a self he has no idea of a self, and hence he has no fear of death. He thinks that even if he is dead he will not be separated from the Bodhisattvas, so he has no fear of an evil destiny. He thinks that there is no one like him with a support in the whole world, much less beyond, and so he has no fear about confidence in assemblies. Thus all fear and terror and stupefaction and hair-raising are gone.

Again the Bodhisattva by putting forward great compassion with unvitiated, special earnestness is still more trained in completely attaining all the roots of goodness.

Lotus, ch. 15.

X. THE BODHISATTVA'S TRAINING

The Bodhisattva begins as an ordinary man who enters upon a high career. He knows that he must pass through many births before attaining his goal, and his way is prepared for him by a ceremony of initiation and by methods of instruction such as given here. The Bodhisattva worshipped by the layman is seen from a very different point of view. The layman looked to the Bodhisattva who has completed his career (often the hero of many legends), and who with his accumulated merits is able to bestow blessings on all who reverence him. Mañjuśrī (or Mañjughoṣa) is one of the mythical Bodhisattvas who like Avalokiteśvara was a popular object of devotion. See *Śāntideva's Prayer*, p. 86.

MAÑJUŚRĪ said to the Lord : how, Lord, ought this discourse of the doctrine to be proclaimed by these Bodhisattvas in the last time, in the last age ? Thereat the Lord said to Mañjuśrī : this discourse ought to be proclaimed by a Bodhisattva who is established in four things. In what four ?

(1) Herein, Mañjuśrī, it should be proclaimed by a Bodhisattva who is established in his sphere of conduct. And how does he become established in his sphere of conduct ? When he becomes patient, subdued, and has attained the stage of being subdued, whose mind is not alarmed and terrified, and is free from impatience, and when he feels no passion for any thing (object), and looks rightly at the real characteristics of things, this absence of discussion and imagination about things is called the conduct of a Bodhisattva.

And what, Mañjuśrī, is the sphere of a Bodhisattva ? When a Bodhisattva does not serve a king, does not serve or attend

upon or reverence or approach kings' sons, ministers or kings'
officers ; when he does not serve or attend upon or reverence
heretics, vagrants, wanderers, professional beggars, Nirgranthas
(Jains), those devoted to poems and learned works ; when he
forms no acquaintance with the repeaters of materialist mantras
not with materialists, does not approach outcasts, boxers, boar-
hunters, poulterers, hunters, butchers, actors, prizefighters,
wrestlers, and those who provide amusements for others nor
form acquaintance with them, except that he speaks the doctrine
to those who approach from time to time and speaks it independently ; when he does not serve or attend or reverence those
of the disciple's career, whether monks, nuns, laymen or lay
women or associate with them, and has not the same sphere of
conduct as they have either in walking or in the way of living,
except that he speaks the doctrine to those who approach him
from time to time, but speaks it independently. This is the
sphere of conduct of a Bodhisattva.

Again, Mañjuśrī, a Bodhisattva does not often, by making
the mutual signs of courtesy, teach the doctrine to a woman,
nor is he often desirous of showing himself to a woman. He
does not visit families, nor does he think that girls, young women
and married women ought to be addressed much, nor does he
return their greeting. He does not teach the doctrine to a
eunuch, nor associate with him nor return his greeting. He
does not enter a house for alms when alone except when meditating in remembrance on the Tathāgata. Again, if he teaches
the doctrine to a woman he does it without any emotion for
the doctrine, to say nothing of emotion for a woman. He does
not in the least show his teeth, to say nothing of any greedy
expression of his mouth. He does not make himself pleasant
to a novice or female novice or monk or nun or boy or girl.
He does not associate with them or make conversation. He is

not inclined to reply, and he does not often keep up a conversation. This is called the first sphere of a Bodhisattva.

(2) Again, Manjuśrī, a Bodhisattva looks upon all things as void.   Comprehending things as truly abiding, as not being perverse, really existent, unmoved, unshakable, not passing away, not evolving, truly abiding, having the nature of space, free from any means of interpretation, unborn, unoriginated, not compounded, not uncompounded, not existent, not non-existent, declared as inexpressible, without existence, not abiding, appearing as not contradicted by perception.[1] Even thus, Manjuśrī, a Bodhisattva often looking upon all things abides. Abiding with this abiding a Bodhisattva is established in his sphere.   This, Manjuśrī, is the second sphere of a Bodhisattva.

(3) Again, Manjuśrī, after the Tathāgata has attained Nirvāṇa, in the last time, in the last age, in the last 500 years, when the good doctrine is disappearing, a Bodhisattva, having the desire to preach this discourse of the doctrine, becomes happily placed, and so preaches the doctrine either from memory or from a book. When he teaches others he is not excessively censorious, nor does he revile other monks who recite the doctrine, or speak blame or impute blame.   He does not take the name of other monks of the Disciple's career and speak blame or impute blame or become an opponent in their presence.   And why ? Because he is happily placed.   He teaches the doctrine without detraction to those who come from time to time to hear the

---

[1] This passage is very corrupt and full of variant readings, but it may be gathered that things in their true nature are being spoken of, and that as such they are indescribable, and that nothing positive in the world of experience can be asserted of them, not even existence, because existence in the real sense is beyond anything that the senses can tell us.

doctrine. He avoids disputes, and when he is asked a question he does not expound it according to the Disciple's career but rather as he is enlightened with Buddha-knowledge.

Again, Mañjuśrī, after the Tathāgata has attained Nirvāṇa, in the last time when the good doctrine is perishing, the Bodhisattva remembering this sūtra is not jealous, not dishonest, not deceitful, and he does not speak blame of other individuals in the Bodhisattva's career. He does not revile them or cause them to be dispirited. And to others, monks, nuns, laymen, or lay women, whether of the career of Disciples. Private Buddhas, or Bodhisattvas, he does not make them feel remorse by saying, "Far away, noble youths, are you from supreme enlightenment, you have not the insight for it, you are abiding in boundless carelessness, you are incapable of being enlightened with that knowledge." In the same way he does not make those in the Bodhisattva career feel remorse. He takes no pleasure in disputes about the doctrine. He does not dispute about the doctrine, nor in the presence of everyone does he omit the power of friendliness. In the presence of all the Tathāgatas he rouses the idea of father, and in the presence of all the Bodhisattvas he rouses the idea of teacher, and he constantly reveres the Bodhisattvas in the ten directions of the universe with intentness and reverence. When teaching the doctrine he teaches neither too little nor too much, with balanced affection for the doctrine, and not to a single person does he show too much favour through his affection for the doctrine, when preaching this discourse.

Equipped with this third principle a Bodhisattva after the Nirvāṇa of the Tathāgata, in the last time when the good doctrine is perishing, while he is preaching this discourse, abides happily, and without being harassed preaches it. In the recital of the doctrine he has companions, and hearers of the doctrine will arise who will hear his discourse, they will hear it, believe it, accept it, learn it, grasp it, write it, cause it to be written, and having recorded it in books will honour it, revere it, laud it, and worship it.

(4) Again, Manjuśrī, a Bodhisattva, after the Nirvāṇa of the Tathāgata, in the last time when the good doctrine is perishing, being desirous of remembering this discourse with the monk, ought to live far away from the presence of householders and wanderers, and he ought to live in a state of friendliness. And in those who have set out the longing ought to be awakened, and thus he ought to rouse their minds : " Verily those beings are of a very little understanding nature who do not listen to the Tathāgata's skill in means spoken in a hidden manner, who do not hear it, do not know it, who have no insight, who do not ask or believe or are not devoted. Truly those beings do not penetrate this discourse or get insight into it. And further again, when I am enlightened with this supreme, perfect enlightenment, through my psychic power I will incline him towards it who has set out for it. I will induce him to accept it, to penetrate it, and I will ripen him." Equipped with this fourth principle, Manjuśrī, a Bodhisattva after the Tathāgata has attained Nirvāṇa, when preaching this discourse becomes free from harm, he is honoured, revered, lauded, and worshipped by monks, nuns, laymen, lay women, kings, princes, ministers, officers, brahmins, and householders.

Lotus, ch. 13.

XI. INITIATION OF A BODHISATTVA

The admission of a monk to the Order consists of two stages, his entrance to the Order on his leaving the world (*pabbajjā*) and, if he is at least twenty years old, his full ordination (*upasampadā*). The whole ceremony of ordination is given in the Vinaya, but as now used it forms a part of the collection of official acts (*kammavācā*).[1]

It is upon this form of proceeding that the following formula for the initiation of a Bodhisattva is based. The original Sanskrit has been published by Dr. N. Dutt (Calcutta, 1931), who says it is called *Bodhisattva-prātimokṣa-sūtra*. This does not explain its actual nature. It is clear that it is a formula for a person undertaking the career of Bodhisattva.

OM. *Reverence to all the Buddhas and Bodhisattvas.*

THE three groups of the moralities of Bodhisattvas have been said to be the morality of self-restraint, the morality of accumulating good actions, and the morality of acting for the welfare of living beings. A householder, or a person that has left the world, who wishes to learn them, and who has made the vow to attain supreme, perfect enlightenment, should make his request at the feet of a Bodhisattva who knows the doctrine, who possesses a great store of merit, and who is able to communicate the word and grasp the meaning.

(The candidate speaks :) " In your presence, noble youth, reverend one or sir,[2] I desire to receive the bestowal of the restraint of the Bodhisattva's morality ; deign therefore to have compassion on me, and without hindrance at once to grant it

---

[1] See translation in *Early Buddhist Scriptures*, ed. by E. J. Thomas, p. 211.

[2] The form of address depends on whether the initiating Bodhisattva is a monk or a layman.

to me and listen." Thus having made his request three times
let him arrange his upper robe on one shoulder, do homage
to the Lord Buddhas of the past, future, and present in the ten
quarters, and to the Bodhisattvas who have entered the Great
Stage, setting their virtues before him ; and producing an
essentially good disposition ; and let him kneel down or crouch
on his haunches, placing an image of the Tathāgata in front
and worshipping and honouring it ; and let him say :

"Grant me, noble youth, reverend one or sir, the bestowal
of the restraint of the Bodhisattva's morality." Then fixing his
attention on one point, let him increase his good disposition,
saying, " Now in no long time shall I attain an imperishable,
immeasurable, supreme, great store of merit." Thus reflecting
on the matter, let him remain silent.

Again, the Bodhisattva who has thus been admitted is to be
addressed by the learned Bodhisattva with undistracted mind,
standing or sitting, thus : " Listen (name of person), noble
youth, reverend one or sir, you are a Bodhisattva, and you have
made your vow to attain enlightenment." He is to reply, OM.

Again, he is to be still further thus addressed : " You (person's name), noble youth, reverend one or sir, you are a Bodhisattva, and in my presence have taken the vow to attain
enlightenment, and are accepting all the Bodhisattva's rules
and all the Bodhisattva's morality, the morality of restraint,
the morality of accumulating good actions, and the morality
of acting for the welfare of living beings ; that which was the
morality of past Bodhisattvas and their moral rules, that which
will be the morality of future Bodhisattvas and their moral
rules, and that which is the morality of present Bodhisattvas
now in the ten quarters and their moral rules ; in the moral
rules and moralities in which all Bodhisattvas of the past have
been instructed, in which all Bodhisattvas of the future will be

instructed, and all Bodhisattvas of the present are being instructed." He is to promise, " This I accept." Three times.

" May the Lord Buddhas and Bodhisattvas assembled in the worlds of the ten quarters pay attention to me. May my teacher pay attention to me. Whatever injury that I (name of person) have committed or caused to be committed or approved of in deed, word, or thought against Buddhas, Bodhisattvas, mother and father, or other beings in this birth or in others, all this I assemble, combine, and ponder in the presence of all Buddhas, Bodhisattvas, and my teacher, and with the best and most real confession I confess it ; and so far as I know and remember I make no concealment." Three times.

" I (person's name) having thus confessed my faults, from this day forth until seated at the Bodhi-tree, go for refuge to the Buddha, the Lord, the greatly compassionate, the omniscient, who has passed beyond all danger of enmity, the great man, of indivisible body, supreme body, dharma-body, chief of men. I (person's name) having thus confessed my faults, from this day forth until seated at the Bodhi-tree, go for refuge to the Dharma, to peace, to the supreme object for those freed from passion. I (person's name) from this day forth until seated at the Bodhi-tree go for refuge to the Order of Bodhisattvas who do not turn back, to the best of companies." Three times.

" I (person's name) having thus confessed my faults, and having gone to the triple refuge, in order to raise and save numberless beings, to rescue them from the pain of transmigration and to establish them in the supreme knowledge of omniscience, as the Bodhisattvas of the past, future, and present having produced the thought of enlightenment have attained, will attain or are attaining Buddhahood, as all the Buddhas with unobstructed Buddha-knowledge and Buddha-vision know and perceive, and as they recognize the non-reality of things, by that rite in the presence of my teacher (name) and before all the Buddhas and Bodhisattvas do I (person's name) produce the thought of supreme, perfect enlightenment." Three times.

" And this root of goodness produced by this confession of faults, by the triple going to the refuge, and by the production of the thought of enlightenment do I transfer to supreme, perfect enlightenment, that in the world which is without refuge, resting-place, goal or resource I may become the rescuing, the refuge, the resting-place, the goal, and the resource ; that I may rescue all unrescued creatures from the ocean of existence ; that I may bring Nirvāṇa to those without Nirvāṇa with unobstructed Nirvāṇa of the elements of things, and that I may console the unconsoled." Three times.

" I (person's name), who have thus caused the thought of enlightenment to arise, accept the infinite world of living beings as my mother, father, sister, brother, son, daughter, and any other blood-relations, and having accepted them as far as is in my power, strength, and knowledge, I cause the roots of goodness to grow in them. From now on, whatever gift I shall give or moral rule I shall keep, or act of patience I shall perform, acting vigorously, or whatever meditation I shall attain, or acting with wisdom shall learn skill in means, all that shall be for the profit and welfare of living beings.

" And having undertaken to win supreme, perfect enlightenment, and having done homage to those Bodhisattvas of great mercy who have entered the Great Stage, I go forth after them. Having gone forth, a Bodhisattva am I, a Bodhisattva. From now on may my teacher support me." Three times.

Then the teacher in front of that image having fallen at the feet of those Buddhas and Bodhisattvas abiding, staying, existing in the ten directions, and having done honour to them, is to announce thus : " This Bodhisattva (person's name) has taken upon himself in the presence of me (person's name) a Bodhisattva, the restraint of the Bodhisattva's morality", down to, "uttering it three times". "I myself (person's name), a Bodhisattva, knowing that I have been an eyewitness, announce to this Bodhisattva (person's name) and to all the most noble beings everywhere who are not present and whose thoughts are not present in the infinite worlds of the ten quarters that in him the restraint of the Bodhisattva's morality has been assumed." Three times.

"Again, as soon as the ceremony of the restraint of morality has been completed, this is the law, that there appears to the Tathāgatas who abide, stay, exist in the infinite worlds in the ten quarters and to the Bodhisattvas who have entered the Great Stage a sign whereby they become aware that a Bodhisattva (person's name) in the presence of a Bodhisattva (person's name) has taken upon him the assumption of the restraint of the Bodhisattva's morality." Thus so far has been declared the rite of assuming (the Bodhisattva's morality).

If an individual having these qualities is not equipped [with a teacher, etc.], then a Bodhisattva before an image of the Tathāgata, on himself assuming the restraint of the Bodhisattva's morality, should thus speak and act: arranging his robe on one shoulder, and having done homage to the past, future, and present Lord Buddhas in the ten quarters and to the Bodhisattvas who have entered the Great Stage, he should put his right knee on the ground or crouch on his haunches and say: "I (person's name) announce to all the Tathāgatas in the ten quarters and to the Bodhisattvas who have entered the Great Stage: before these I undertake all the Bodhisattva's rules and all the Bodhisattva's morality, the morality", as before, down to,[1] "a Bodhisattva am I, a Bodhisattva. From now on may the Lord Buddhas and Bodhisattvas support me." Thus the announcement.

[1] The announcement in the full rite is made by the teacher, where the words here omitted will be found, pp. 56–58.

XII. THE BODHISATTVA'S CONFESSION

The following from the *Golden Splendour sūtra* is not a part of the Bodhisattva's ceremony of initiation, but the outpouring of a heart intent on its lofty aim. The original is in verse, but the translation has been made quite literal.

MAY the Buddhas deign to notice me,
With minds full of pity and compassion;
Established in the ten quarters
May they take away my transgression.

The sinful action, the fearful deeds,
That I have done aforetime,
All that will I confess,
Standing before the Buddhas.

The sin that has been done by me
Through despising mother and father,
Through not understanding the Buddhas,
And through not understanding the good;

The sin that has been done by me
Intoxicated with the madness of lordship,
With the madness of family pride,
Intoxicated with the madness of youth;

The sin that has been done by me,
The evil thought and evil speech,
Together with action badly done,
Through not seeing their wretchedness;

Through practising foolish thoughts,
Through my mind being wrapped in ignorance,
Through the influence of bad friends,
Through my mind being blurred with the depravities;

The sin of deed, of word, of thought,
The threefold wickedness that I have done,
Whatever I have committed in such ways,
All that do I confess.

The disrespect that I have shown
To the Buddhas and their doctrines,
And likewise to the disciples,
All that do I confess.

Whatever disrespect I have shown
To the Pratyekabuddhas,
Or again to the Bodhisattvas,
All that do I confess.

If the good Doctrine has been reviled
By me ever through my ignorance,
Disrespect to mother and father,
All that do I confess.

What I have done through folly and ignorance
Through being wrapped in conceit and pride,
Through passion, hate, and stupidity,
All that do I confess.

In the ten quarters of the world,
Having worshipped the Victors with the ten powers,
Creatures will I extricate
In the ten quarters from all pain.

Upon the tenth stage will I set
All beings inconceivably many;
And standing on the tenth stage
All shall become Tathāgatas . . .

Through hundreds of thousands of concentrations,
Through spells inconceivably many,
Through the faculties, the powers, and parts of enlightenment
May I become a supreme Buddha.

May the Buddhas look upon me
With attentive minds;
May they take away my transgression.
May they release me from danger.

The sin that has been done aforetime
By me through hundreds of cycles,
On that account my mind grieves,
Wretched am I, afflicted by craving.

I fear; for sinful are my deeds;
Ever am I base-minded;
Wherever I may wander
There is no good fortune.

May all the compassionate Buddhas,
The Victors who release beings from danger,
Take away my transgression.
And release me from danger.

The fruit of my depraved deeds
May the Tathāgatas bear away;
And may the Buddhas bathe me
With the pure waters of their compassion.

I desire to confess all my sin,
Which aforetime I have committed;
And now indeed that sin of mine
All of it do I confess.

For the future every sin that I commit,
Every action wrongly done,
That sin do I not conceal,
Whatever may my wrong action be.

The threefold action of the body,
The fourfold action of speech,
The threefold action of the mind,
All that do I confess.

That action done by the body, by speech,
And meditated by the mind,
Action done in the ten ways,
All that do I confess.

Avoiding the ten bad actions,
Pursuing the ten good actions,
I will stand on the tenth stage,
And behold the supreme Buddha.

The sinful action done by me
That brings unwished-for fruit,
All that will I confess,
Standing before the Buddhas.

And those that dwell in the Rose-apple land,
And those in other world-regions,
Who do good actions,
May they approve all this.

The virtuous action done by me
Through deed and word and thought,
By that root of goodness
May I attain supreme enlightenment.

Suvarṇaprabhāsa-s, ch. 4.

XIII. THE BODHISATTVA'S DUTIES

The *Śikṣāsamuccaya*, " Compendium of Instruction ", is a work by Śāntideva consisting of 27 verses, on each of which he has written his own commentary with many quotations from Mahāyāna texts. Two of them are here given, the first on the particular duties which the Bodhisattva must fulfil during his career, and the other expressing the Bodhisattva's aspirations when he first makes his vow.

THE great being who has thus heard and who has also with wisdom penetrated the difficult practice of the Bodhisattva's career, and who is also able to bear the burden of rescuing all afflicted beings should first (1) perform salutation (to the Buddhas), (2) do reverence to them, (3) make confession of sin, (4) rejoice in the performance of virtue, (5) exhort Buddhas to preach and implore them to delay their Nirvāṇa, (6) produce the thought of enlightenment, (7) transfer to others the merit of his good deeds, and (8) should approach a good friend, repeating (the vow) after him or uttering it himself, and should say, " Consider, teacher, I (person's name)", and should produce the thought of enlightenment, as was done by the Lord Manjuśrī, for he spoke thus :

> As far as the farthest bound unceasing
> Of transmigration extends,
> So far for the good of creatures
> Will I practise the limitless career.
>
> May we produce the thought of enlightenment
> In the presence of our leader ;
> All the world do I invite ;
> From poverty will I release it.

No thought of the vice of malice
Or envy or of jealousy
From today onward will I maintain,
Until I reach enlightenment.

Continence will I practise,
And evil lusts will I renounce ;
In the moral restraints and rules
Of the Buddhas will I become trained.

Not in a hurried manner here
Have I power to win enlightenment ;
Within the limit of existence will I stand
For one single being's sake.

An immeasurable, inconceivable
Buddha-field will I purify ;
And I will make my name
Renowned in the ten quarters.

In deeds of body and speech
I will make myself pure in every way ;
I will purify the deed of my mind
Nor will I do a sinful action.

Śikṣāsamuccaya, p. 13.

XIV. DECAY OF THE DOCTRINE

In the Pāli Scriptures Buddha is said to have prophesied that the Doctrine would last a thousand years, but that if women were admitted to the Order it would not last more than five hundred. This sense of transitoriness and decay seems to have increased, as may be seen from the previous chapter, and in the present passage the fear of degeneration both in doctrine and discipline is still more vividly expressed.

BUDDHA speaks : Such were my first practices, when I was formerly practising austerities ; nor was there then in my mind any distress while I was seeking enlightenment.

There was nothing within or without that I did not give ; in morality, patience, and courage, in meditation, skill in means, and wisdom was I practised.

My flesh, skin, marrow, and blood I gave from my own body ; when I was in deserts and caves my body dried up as I practised.

The way of hard penance taught by the Buddhas, wherein the Buddhas become exercised, in this hard penance I was ever being exercised, and formerly practising it constantly.

Such were the lofty vows that I followed as I practised ; and some there will be who having heard the marvel will not at once be roused to delight.

There will be laughter when they hear it, even as now at my teaching ; they will be intent on carousing and debauchery, ever overcome by sloth, filled with hundreds of longings.

Enemies of the doctrine, ever ignoble, corrupters of the teaching, deprived of every virtue ; and on hearing this tranquil doctrine they will declare it was not uttered by the Buddha.

They will say, " My teacher was an ocean of learning, very

learned was he, the best of speakers ; this was disallowed by
him, this is not at all the Buddha-word.

" Further, he had an old tutor who had mastered a flood of
virtues ; yet this was not held by him ; do not exercise yourself
therein, it is false.

" Where it is taught that there is no self, no life-principle,
effort there becomes useless and also the exercise of morality
and the practice of restraint.

" And if there is this Mahāyāna, and in it no self, no creature,
no human being is admitted, then is it useless for me to make
effort, when neither self nor creature is recognized.

" These are rhapsodies, the individual views of men of evil
doctrine and the followers of base heretics ; the Buddha would
never have uttered that speech, a slandering of the monks."

Void of modesty, shame, and virtue, impudent as crows,
haughty, impetuous will be the monks of my teaching, con-
sumed with envy, pride, and infatuation.

Agitating their hands and feet, shaking the corners of their
dress, with yellow robes on their necks they will go about
among village families and get drunk with liquor.

They take the Buddha's banner (the robe), and pay court to
householding people ; they always take some doctrinal writing,
but neglect the accumulating of merit.

Through gifts of oxen, asses, horses, and cattle they become
enslaved ; with their minds applied to the business of farming
and trading they are ever ignoble.

For them no speech is ignoble, nor is there anything that
ought not to be done ; wealth of shrines or of the Order or of
individuals—to them it is all the same.

And if they notice among them a monk rich in virtue, they
speak in his dispraise ; they become vicious, deceitful, and
hypocritical, and these dreadful creatures corrupt women.

As householders through their desires are lustful, so will these monks be lustful ; they will have wives and sons and daughters just like householders.

Even in a family where they are honoured with the boons of robes and alms they will be lustful for the wife, slaves of their passions, ever ignoble.

"These lusts are not to be followed ; they lead to rebirth as animals, ghosts, and in the hells" ; so will they constantly say to the householders, yet they themselves are neither disciplined nor calmed.

And as they themselves are undisciplined, so too their troop of disciples will not be well disciplined ; by night and day they will indulge in carousing, debauchery, and gossip.

It is for the sake of honour, not virtue, that they form a troop of disciples (and say), "Attended by my own group of pupils I shall ever succeed in receiving worship here among the people".

And among the people they say, "This is my troop ; out of compassion for it I do not ask service at any time from this my group of pupils".

Overcome by diseases, leprous, with spotted limbs, misshapen, they will wander in the hells, born again and again, ever ignoble.

Devoid of the restraint of the Rule, ever without the monk's virtues, they are neither householders nor monks ; they are shunned like a block of wood in a cemetery.

They will have no respect for the rules of the novices nor the monks' rules nor the Discipline ; without self-control they will follow their own wishes, like elephants freed from the goad.

Though dwelling in the forest they will have their thoughts on going to the village ; fallen into the fire of the passions their thought will not be fixed.

Forgetting all the Buddha-virtues, the strict precepts and the means, filled with infatuation, pride, and conceit, they fall into the dreadful Avīchī hell.

Ever delighting in tales of kings, in tales and descriptions of robbers, they take pleasure in serving their relatives, full of brooding by day and night.

Neglecting meditation and study, ever bent on the affairs of the monastery, they will frown at the vultures that dwell there, attended by undisciplined pupils.

" I am not a workman in the monastery ; it has been made for my sake ; only those monks that are agreeable to me have occasion to be in the monastery."

As for those of good morals and virtuous, who know the Doctrine by heart, and are intent on the welfare of creatures, who are ever trained in self-control and restraint, he never takes his troop from among those.

" That has been assigned to me as my place, that belongs to my fellow monk, and that to my companion ; go, there is no place for you to live here.

" All the beds and seats have been distributed ; many monks are established here ; there is nothing here for you to gain ; what are you going to eat here ? Depart, monk."

But for them there will be no assigning of beds and seats at any time ; they will have stores like householders, and be equipped with abundant requisites.

And my sons will be wholly put to shame in the last time ; without remembering my word they will dwell in border forests.

Alas ! the teaching of the best of Buddhas will not be long in going to destruction, when many monks appear who are slaves to gain and hostile to virtue.

And they in the last time, who are devoted to morals and virtue, will be ever despised ; and they will dwell in the forests, avoiding villages and towns.

The rest, honoured but without virtue, will be eager for dissension, lovers of disputes ; accounted learned by the people, they will be eaten up with pride and infatuation.

This teaching of mine, a hoard of virtues, a mine of all virtues, supremely delightful, will go to destruction ; morals will be ruined through the vices of envy and infatuation.

Like a pillaged mine of jewels, like a dried-up lotus-pool, like a shattered pillar of finest gems, my teaching will perish in the last time.

Let him to whom are dear the Buddha, the noble Order, and the disciple's strict rules, thus ever apply himself and abandon mere knowledge, gain, and honour.

As an illusion and as a dream should compound things be regarded ; in no long time will there be separation from all things pleasant ; here nought is permanent.

Ever practise and be active in the Perfections, the Stages, and the Powers ; and never fail in courage until the attainment of supreme enlightenment.

Rāṣṭrapāla-paripṛcchā, 27.

XV. BODHISATTVA WORSHIP

The earlier Mahāyāna discourses portray the Bodhisattva in his career to win enlightenment and to bestow the benefit of his merits on numberless beings. Hence among the laity the Bodhisattvas became rivals of the Hindu tutelary gods. There was probably direct Hindu influence, for a Sarvāstivādin story tells of a Hindu who wished to buy a lotus to offer to his god in opposition to a Buddhist, who wished to offer it to Buddha. Discourses were composed in which the main subject was not doctrine, but the marvellous achievements of such beings. One of the best known is the *Kāraṇḍavyūha*, which tells how Avalokiteśvara went to the lowest hell to cool it, relieved those suffering as ghosts, took them to Sukhāvatī, and even assumed the form of a brahmin in order to preach to the gods of the Pure abode.

THUS have I heard : at one time the Lord dwelt at Śrāvasti at the Jetavana monastery in the park of Anāthapiṇḍada with a great assembly of monks, with 1,200 monks and many hundred thousands of Bodhisattvas. (The names of twenty are given followed by long lists of classes of gods and goddesses, and ending with " many hundred thousands of Jains ".)

When the great assembly took place rays issued from the great hell of Avīchī, and on issuing they reached the Jetavana monastery. Everything in the monastery appeared adorned. The pillars appeared inlaid and adorned with precious stones, the pinnacles covered with gold, and in each house the doors were of gold and silver . . .

Now in that assembly the Bodhisattva, the great being named Sarvanīvaraṇavishkambhin arose from his seat, arranged his upper robe on one shoulder, placed his right knee on the ground, and bowing with folded hands to the Lord, said to the Lord, " I am filled with marvel and wonder, Lord ; whence have these rays come ? Of what Tathāgata is this the special majesty?" The Lord said, "This is not the majesty of a Tathāgata, noble youth. The noble Avalokiteśvara, the Bodhisattva, the great being, has entered into the hell Avīchī,[1] and after having released beings there he is entering the city of ghosts. Hence have the rays been emitted."

So the Bodhisattva said to the Lord, "Lord, what beings are there in Avīchī? Where no wave is recognizable does he there teach his doctrine? Where surrounded by walls and ramparts the ground is of iron, blazing up with one continuous flame, and flashing like a casket of jewels, and in this great hell stands a roaring cauldron, and into it are thrown many hundred thousands of crores of millions of beings; as beans or pulse going up and down in a pot full of water sweating and seething are cooked, so these beings in the great hell of Avīchī suffer bodily pain. How then, Lord, does Avalokiteśvara enter into the great hell of Avīchī?"

The Lord said, "Just as, noble youth, a universal king enters his park of divine jewels in the great prosperity of universal kingship, even so does Avalokiteśvara enter the great hell of Avīchī. Nor again does he go in any other shape. When he draws near to the great hell of Avīchī, then it becomes cool. Then Death's guardians are agitated in mind and fall into the greatest distress of mind, wondering what inauspicious sign has appeared in the great hell. When Avalokiteśvara enters, then lotuses the size of a cartwheel appear therein, and the cauldron bursts asunder. In the place of the fire a lotus-pool appears.

Then Death's guardians seizing swords, pestles, javelins, maces, clubs, wheels, tridents, and other weapons, and taking the whole paraphernalia of Avīchī went to Death (Yama), the king of Dharma, and said to him, "Let the god first know this, that our sphere of action is utterly destroyed, and has become

[1] The lowest of the hells.

pleasant and full of all happiness." Death replied, " What is
the reason that your sphere of action is destroyed ? " Death's
guardians said, " Let the god first know this, that in this great
hell of Avīchī an inauspicious sign has appeared. Everything
has become calm and cool, and a beautiful man has entered,
wearing a diadem on his matted hair, his mind filled with the
highest friendliness, and looking like a disc of gold. Such a
man has entered here, and when he merely entered there
appeared lotuses the size of cart-wheels, and the cauldron burst
asunder. In the place of the fire a lotus-pool has appeared."

Then the thought occurred to Death, the king of Dharma,
" Now of what god is this the majesty ? Is it that of Maheśvara
(Śiva) the god with great magic powers ? Or that of Nārāyaṇa
(Krishṇa) worshipped by the five great oceans ? Or has some
special result through a gift of power taken place in others of
the gods of great magic ·power, and they have arrived in this
region ? Or has a rākshasa come ? Is it a rival of the great
Rāvaṇa ? " Thus did he stand there reflecting, and as he looked
with his divine eye he was not able to see among the host of
gods any other whose power it might be. So he looked again
into the great hell of Avīchī, and on looking in he saw Avalokiteśvara, the Bodhisattva, the great being.

So Death, the king of Dharma, approached Avalokiteśvara,
and on approaching him he saluted the Lord's feet with his head,
and began to utter an excellent hymn of praise :

" Reverence to Avalokiteśvara, to Maheśvara,[1] to Padmaśrī,
the giver of boons, the fulfiller of wishes, the giver of excellent
sight to the earth, the consoler of the world, the hundred-
thousand-armed, with a hundred thousand crores of eyes, with

[1] This is also the usual name of the god Śiva, but this god is quite distinct
from the Bodhisattva, as he is introduced later on in this sūtra as a wor-
shipper of Avalokiteśvara.

eleven heads, who extends down to the marine fire, to whom the
doctrine is dear, releaser of all beings, consoler of the tortoises,
sharks, and fishes (of transmigration), completer of the sum of
knowledge, giver of favours, supreme drier-up of Avīchī,
adorner of the grace of knowledge, to whom knowledge is
dear, worshipped and revered and adored by all the gods,
bestower of safety, bestower of the doctrine, expounder of the
six Perfections, maker of the sight of the sun, illuminator of the
doctrine, assuming forms at will, assuming the form of a celestial
musician, ascender of the golden mountain, whose doctrine is
profound as the bosom of the ocean, who has attained the practice of the highest meaning, who is endowed with many hundred
thousand forms of concentration, joy-maker, with anointed
limbs, maker of heroic sages, releaser from the way of fear and
terror of the bonds and fetters of the heart, united with the
non-being of all creatures, with a great retinue, maker of
increase, wishing jewel, instructor of the way to Nirvāṇa,
drier-up of the city of ghosts, maker of the umbrella of the
world, releaser from sicknesses, sacred thread of the sacrifice
performed by the serpent-kings Nanda and Upananda, endowed
with many hundreds of spells, who puts the thunderbolt-bearer
to flight, who produces safety in the three worlds, who terrifies
yakshas, rākṣasas, spirits, ghosts, vampires, she-goblins, abor-
tions, having fair blue lotus-eyes, of profound firmness.   Lord
of knowledge, releaser from all the depravities, who in various
ways increases the way to enlightenment, the chief of those who
have entered the way of release, who increases the way of
enlightenment with the thought of the support, endowed with
hundreds of thousands of concentrations like atomic dust."

Thus Death, the king of Dharma, having uttered a very
excellent hymn of devotion, passed three times round to the
right and went away.   *Kāraṇḍavyūha.*

XVI. THE MERITS OF AVALOKITEŚVARA

The conclusion of this passage shows the error of supposing that existence in Sukhāvatī means the attainment of final bliss. In that universe they listen to the instruction of Amitābha until they have acquired the omniscience of a Buddha.

THEN Sarvanīvaraṇavishkambhin said to the Lord, " Lord, is Avalokiteśvara, the Bodhisattva, the great being, not coming here today ? " The Lord said, " Noble youth, he is ripening many hundred thousands of crores of millions of beings. Day by day he comes and ripens them. There is no such splendour even of Tathāgatas as of Avalokiteśvara, the Bodhisattva, the great being." " In what way, Lord ? " The Lord said, " In former times, noble youth, a Tathāgata, an arhat, a perfectly enlightened Buddha arose in the world named Vipaśvin,[1] endowed with knowledge and conduct, Sugata, knower of the world, a supreme charioteer of men to be tamed, a teacher of gods and men, Buddha, Lord. At that time and period I was a merchant's son named Sugandhamukha. Then I heard from the Tathāgata Vipaśvin of the virtues produced by Avalokiteśvara, the Bodhisattva, the great being." " What, Lord, was the production of virtues like, of which you heard, what was it like ? May the Lord declare to me, what the production of these virtues was like."

The Lord said, " From his eyes arose the moon and sun,[2] from his forehead Maheśvara (Śiva), from his shoulders Brahmā,

---

[1] This was the first of the six Buddhas before Sakyamuni.

[2] This was at the beginning of a cycle, when the universe begins to evolve again. In Hinduism Vishnu is usually the creator, and his functions are here ascribed to Avalokiteśvara.

from his heart Nārāyaṇa, from his teeth Sarasvatī, from his mouth the winds, from his feet the earth, and from his belly Varuṇa. When these gods were born from the body of Avalokiteśvara, then he said to the god Maheśvara, 'Thou shalt be Maheśvara in the Kali age, when the world of evil creatures arises. Thou shalt be called Ādideva (the primal god), the creator, the maker. All beings shall be deprived of the way of enlightenment who give such an account among the common people.' (A long description of other virtues of Avalokiteśvara follows.) But, noble youth, it is not possible to count the collection of the merits of Avalokiteśvara, the Bodhisattva. For example, noble youth, I can count each single leaf in a forest of acacia trees, but I am not able to count the collection of the merits of Avalokiteśvara. For example, noble youth, if in the four continents all the women, men, boys, and girls were to be set in the stage of the fruit of entering the stream, the fruit of Once-returner, the fruit of Non-returner, arhatship, or private Buddhahood, their merits would be surpassed by the collection of the merits of Avalokiteśvara."

Then Ratnapāṇi the Bodhisattva, the great being, said to the Lord, "I have nowhere seen or heard, Lord, of such an inconceivable collection of merits of Tathāgatas, much less of a Bodhisattva, like the collection of merits of the Lord Avalokiteśvara."

The Lord said, "There might be Tathāgatas, arhats, perfect Buddhas like me, as numerous as the sands of the Ganges, staying in one place to be honoured with robes, bowls, couches, vehicles, medicines, and requisites fit for the gods, and all of them assembled together could not count the collection of merits of Avalokiteśvara, much less, noble youth, I who dwell singly in this universe—how can I utter in speech the collection of his merits? And also, noble youth, all Tathāgatas with ten utterances have said, ' Those beings become happy in the world who remember the name of Avalokiteśvara, the Bodhisattva, the great being ; they become released from old age, death, sickness, grief, lamentation, pain, and dejection ; they suffer not the unending pain of transmigration ; robed in pure white, like royal geese flying with the speed of the wind, they go to the universe of Sukhāvatī to hear the doctrine face to face with the Tathāgata Amitābha, and having heard the doctrine the pain of transmigration no longer torments their bodies ; nor do lust, hatred, illusion, old age, and death, nor the pains of hunger and thirst torment their bodies ; nor do they remember the pain of abiding in a womb ; there they are born in a lotus.   They abide in that universe as long as the firm promise of Avalokiteś-vara is not fulfilled, that all beings are to be released from all pains, as long as they are not established in supreme, perfect enlightenment.' "

Kāraṇḍavyūha, p. 14.

XVII. THE SPELL OF THE PERFECTION
OF WISDOM

The doctrines of one of the Mahāyāna schools are contained in a number of works all called " The Perfection of Wisdom ". They are of very different length, and the shorter ones are sometimes mistakenly said to be abbreviations of the longest, but although they all have the same teaching they are each of them independent compositions. They all teach dogmatically the voidness or unreality of individual things, and in the following form it has been compressed into a bare statement of the voidness of all things and adapted for use as a spell. For older Buddhism all things were embraced in the five groups constituting the individual, the *skandhas* and the *dhātus*, " elements ", things as perceived by the six senses.

THE noble Avalokiteśvara while practising his practice in the profound Perfection of Wisdom observed : there are five groups (*skandhas*), and he observed them as void of reality.

Here, Sāriputra, body is voidness, voidness is body. Voidness is not separate from body, body is not separate from voidness. What is body, that is voidness. What is voidness, that is body. And so sensation, perception, the *sanskāras* (the other mental elements), and consciousness.

Here, Sāriputra, all things have the mark of voidness, they are unoriginated, not ceased, spotless, not unspotted, not incomplete, not complete. Therefore, Sāriputra, in voidness there is no body, no sensation, no perception, no *sanskāras*, no consciousness, no sight, hearing, smelling, tasting, touching, mind.

No eye-element, down to mind-element.

No knowledge, no ignorance, no destruction of knowledge, no destruction of ignorance [here follow the other links of the

Chain of Causation] down to old age and death, no destruction of old age and death, no arising and ceasing of pain, no Way, no knowledge, no obtaining.

Supported on the Perfection of Wisdom of a Bodhisattva one abides with obstruction of mind. With the non-existence of the obstruction of mind one is free from fear, having passed beyond perverseness, with Nirvāṇa established.

All the Buddhas of the three times supported on the Perfection of Wisdom have become enlightened with supreme, perfect enlightenment.

Therefore the great spell (*mantra*), the Perfection of Wisdom, should be known, the great spell of knowledge, the supreme spell, the incomparable spell, which calms all pains, because it is true and not false. The spell in the Perfection of Wisdom has been spoken, namely :

> *Gate gate pāragate pārasaṃgate bodhi svāhā.*

O gone, gone, gone to the other shore, arrived at the other shore, O enlightenment, svāhā.

XVIII. THE HAPPY UNIVERSE

Each universe forms the "Buddha-field" or sphere of action of only one Buddha. The best known of the other universes is Sukhāvatī, sometimes translated "the happy land", and known to Japanese scholars as "Pure Land", the name of the school (*Jodo* or *Zio-do*) which bases its teaching chiefly on this discourse, *Sukhāvatī-vyūha*. It is west of the universe of Sakyamuni, which is known as Sahā.[1] It is only one of innumerable universes, but it has become prominent owing to its being described in several sūtras and through its becoming connected with the Bodhisattva Avalokiteśvara. This Bodhisattva transfers his own merits to those who call upon him, so that they are reborn in Sukhāvatī. Existence in this universe is not final salvation, but through the merits of Avalokiteśvara they stay there listening to the preaching of the Buddha Amitābha or Amitāyus until they attain complete enlightenment.

THUS have I heard : at one time the Lord dwelt at Śrāvastī in the Jetavana monastery, in the park of Anāthapiṇḍada with a great assembly of monks, with 1,250 monks, who had acquired the higher knowledges, elders, great disciples, all of them arhats, namely, the elder Sāriputra, the great Maudgalyāyana, the great Kāśyapa, the great Kapphiṇa, the great Kātyāyana, the great Kauṣṭhila, Revata, Cūḍyapanthaka, Nanda, Ānanda, Rāhula, Gavāmpati, Bharadvāja, Kālodāyin, Vakkula, and Aniruddha, and with these many other great disciples ; and many Bodhisattvas, great beings, namely Manjuśrī Kumārabhūta, Ajita, Gandha-hastin, Nityodyukta, Aniksiptadhura, and many other Bodhi-

[1] *Sahā* is interpreted as "world of patience or suffering", but as Przyluski has shown, it has been evolved from *Sahāmpati*, a title of Brahmā, which really means "Lord of the assembly", *Sahā* being a Prākrit form of *sabhā*.

sattvas, great beings ; also with Śakra, king of the gods, Brahmā Sahāmpati, and many other hundred thousand millions of gods.

Then the Lord addressed the elder Sāriputra : there is, Sāriputra, in the western quarter from here, passing beyond a hundred thousand crores of Buddha-fields, a Buddha-field named the Universe Sukhāvatī. There the Tathāgata, the arhat, the perfect Buddha named Amitāyus now abides, dwells, lives, and teaches the doctrine. What do you think, Sāriputra, what is the reason why that universe is called the Happy ? Further, in that Happy universe, Sāriputra, beings have no pain of body or pain of mind, but the causes of happiness are immeasurable. For that reason the universe is called the Happy.

Again, Sāriputra, the Happy universe is adorned with seven terraces, seven rows of palm trees with network of hills, all overlaid, varied and lovely with the four precious things, namely, gold, silver, lapis lazuli, and crystal. With such arrangement of the qualities of Buddha-fields is that Buddha-field adorned.

Again, Sāriputra, in the Happy universe are lotus-pools of the seven precious things, namely, of gold, silver, lapis lazuli, crystal, red pearl, emerald, and coral as the seventh. They are full of water of the eight qualities, have even landing places, with water to the brim, and are strewn with golden sand, but in those pools at each of the four sides are four flights of steps, varied and lovely with the four precious things, namely, gold, silver, lapis lazuli, and crystal. And all round the pools grow trees varied and lovely with the seven precious things. And in the pools grow lotuses, blue, blue-coloured, displaying blue, showing blue, yellow, red, white, mixed, the size of a cartwheel. With such arrangement of the qualities of Buddha-fields is that Buddha-field adorned.

Again, Sāriputra, in that Budda-field divine musical instruments ever sound, and the earth is gold-coloured and pleasant.

And in that Buddha-field three times at night and three times in the daytime a rain of divine mandārava flowers falls. And there the beings who are born there go to other universes before their early meal and salute hundreds of thousands of crores of Buddhas, and having sprinkled each Tathāgata with hundreds of thousands of crores of showers of flowers they come back again to their own universe for their period (of meditating) in the open air. With such arrangement of the qualities of Buddha-fields is that Buddha-field adorned.

Again, Sāriputra, in that Buddha-field are geese, herons, and peacocks. They flock together three times at night and three times in the daytime and make a chanting together, each producing its own note. When they produce it they utter the words of the faculties, powers, and parts of enlightenment. When the human beings there hear those words, the reflexion on the Buddha, the Doctrine, and the Order arises in them. Do you think, Sāriputra, that those are creatures who have been born as animals? Not thus should it be regarded. And why? In that Buddha-field, Sāriputra, there is not even the name of hells or of creatures born as animals, or the world of Yama (the god of death). These flocks of birds have been produced by the Tathāgata Amitāyus, and utter the word 'Doctrine'. With such arrangement of the qualities of Buddha-fields is that Buddha-field adorned. (The same is said of the sounds coming from the hells.)

What do you think, Sāriputra, for what reason is that Tathāgata called Amitāyus? Now the length of life of that Tathāgata and of those human beings is immeasurable.[1] For that reason is that Tathāgata called Amitāyus, and ten cycles have passed, Sāriputra, since that Tathāgata was enlightened with supreme, perfect enlightenment.

[1] *Amita*, 'unmeasured', *āyus*, 'life'.

What do you think, Sāriputra, for what reason is that Tathā-gata called Amitābha ?   Now the light (*ābhā*) of that Tathāgata is unhindered in all Buddha-fields.   For that reason is this Buddha called Amitābha, and he has an assembly of disciples, of whom it is not easy to reckon the extent of the faithful arhats.

Again, Sāriputra, of those beings who have been born in the Buddha-field of the Tathāgata Amitāyus, pure Bodhisattvas, not to be turned back, bound by only one birth, it is not easy to reckon the extent except by saying they are immeasurable. Now again beings should make the vow to attain that Buddha-field.   And for what reason ?   To be where there is association with that kind of good persons.   It is not on account of a minor root of merit, Sāriputra, that beings are born in the Buddha-field of the Tathāgata Amitāyus.   Any noble youth or noble daughter who shall hear the name of the Lord Amitāyus, the Tathāgata, and having heard it shall reflect upon it, and for one night, or two, three, four, five, six or seven nights and shall reflect upon it with undistracted mind, when that noble youth or noble daughter comes to die, at the time of his death the Tathāgata Amitāyus attended by an assembly of disciples and a troop of Bodhisattvas will stand before him, and he will die with uncon-fused mind, and on dying will be reborn in the Buddha-field of the Tathāgata Amitāyus, in the Happy Universe.   Therefore now, Sāriputra, considering the force of the matter I say thus, that a noble youth or noble daughter acting with respect should make in his mind the vow to attain to that Buddha-field.

(Buddha then mentions the Buddhas of the four quarters, nadir, and zenith, who are " equal in number to the sands of the Ganges ", and who, like him, are praising it.)

What do you think, Sāriputra, for what reason is this discourse of the doctrine called " the Receiving of all the Buddhas " ? Those noble youths or noble daughters, who shall hear the name of this discourse and shall bear in mind the names of those Lord Buddhas, shall all be received by those Buddhas and be destined not to turn back from attaining supreme, perfect enlightenment. Therefore now, Sāriputra, believe, accept, and do not doubt me and these Lord Buddhas. Those noble sons or noble daughters who shall make in their minds the vow to attain to the Buddha-field of the Lord Amitāyus, the Tathāgata, or who have done so, or who are now doing so, shall be destined not to turn back from supreme, perfect enlightenment, and they shall be reborn in that Buddha-field, or have been reborn, or are being reborn there. Therefore, now, Sāriputra, faithful noble youths and noble daughters should cause the vow to arise in their minds to attain that Buddha-field.

And just as, Sāriputra, I am now praising the qualities so inconceivable of those Lord Buddhas, even so, Sāriputra, are those Lord Buddhas also praising my qualities so inconceivable, saying, " A very hard thing has been done by the Lord Sakya-muni, the Sakya king. Having attained supreme, perfect enlightenment in the Saha universe he has taught the doctrine that is in opposition to the whole world in this corruption of the cycle, corruption of beings, corruption of views, corruption of life, and corruption of the depravities." And this supremely hard thing, Sāriputra, has been done by me, that having attained supreme, perfect enlightenment in the Saha universe I have taught the doctrine that is in opposition to the whole world, in the corruption of beings, corruption of views, corruption of the depravities, corruption of life, and corruption of the cycle.

Thus said the Lord, delighted the elder Sāriputra, the monks, and the Bodhisattvas together with the world of gods, men, asuras, and celestial musicians, praised the words of the Lord.

Smaller Sukhāvatī-vyūka.

XIX. ŚĀNTIDEVA'S PRAYER

Śāntideva was a Bodhisattva of India in the 7th century A.D. His poem, *Bodhicaryāvatāra*, "Introduction to the Practice of Enlightenment", is not part of the Scriptures, but this portion is given here, as it shows the ideal of the career still flourishing. It also illustrates the two features mentioned above, the toilsome career of the Bodhisattva and the belief in the great beings who have achieved it.

THROUGH this auspicious work of mine may all people become adorned with the practice of enlightenment.

May all those in all the directions who are pained by ills of body and mind, win through my merits oceans of happiness and joy.

Through all the changes of transmigration may their happiness never wane ; unceasingly may the world win the happiness of Bodhisattvas.

Whatever hells there are in the universes, may the beings in them rejoice in the happiness and joy of the happy universe, Sukhāvatī.

May those pained by cold become warm, and those pained by heat become cool through the oceans of water shed by the great rain-clouds of Bodhisattvas.

May the Forest of Swords become for them the splendour of the heavenly Nandana grove ; and may the thorny cotton-trees [1] grow into wishing-trees.

---

[1] The forest of swords and the cotton-trees are forms of torture in the hells. Nandana was a grove in the heaven of the god Indra.

May the depths of hell become delightful and fair with the sounds of geese, ducks, mallards, and such birds, and with lotus-pools scented with splendid lotuses . . .

Death's guardians and the crows and vultures terrified shall suddenly see the darkness vanish, saying, "Whose glory is this that spreads happiness and delight all round?" Looking upwards they behold Vajrapāṇi blazing in the sky, and with a thrill of joy their evil destiny therewith passes away.

A rain of lotuses falls mingled with scented water; O blessing! it is seen quenching the fire of hell; what thing is this? Shall not the beings of hell exult with joy, when suddenly the sight of one with a lotus in his hand appears?

"Come, come quickly, cast away fear, O brothers, we are made to live; he is ours who makes the fire afraid, a young man who wears dark garments, through whose might all calamity is gone; the activities of joy have arisen; the thought of enlightenment is born, the mother who saves all people, the compassionate one.

Would that you, friends, may see him, the lotus of his feet honoured by the tiaras of hundreds of gods, his eyes moist with tears of compassion, and fallen on his head is a streaming rain of many flowers. On lovely terraces thousands of goddesses chant their hymns of praises on seeing Manjughosha; may there now be a response from the beings of hell.

Thus through my merits may the beings of hell behold and rejoice at the clouds of Bodhisattvas all round led by Samanta-bhadra, which rain with a pleasantly cool and odorous breeze.

May the ghosts ever be sated and bathed, and made cool by the streams of milk flowing from the hands of the noble Avalokiteśvara.

May there be health for the sick, may prisoners be released from all bonds ; may the weak become strong, may beings become kindly to one another.

May all the directions become auspicious for all that travel on the road ; and may the purpose for which they journey be successful.

May those who have embarked on a ship or mounted a car succeed in their wishes ; may they reach their family in peace and take their pleasure with their kinsfolk.

May those who have lost their way in the forest light upon a caravan ; may they go without fatigue, and not in fear of robbers or tigers.

To those who are asleep, intoxicated or careless, in stress of sickness or in the jungle, to orphans, children, or aged persons, may the gods give protection.

May beings ever have the society of Buddhas and sons of Buddhas ; and with boundless clouds of worship may they worship the Teacher of the world.

May the god rain in season, and the harvest be prosperous ; may the people be wealthy and the king righteous.

May remedies be efficacious, may the spells of those who mutter them succeed ; may the female demons, goblins, and such creatures be filled with pity.

May there be no being in pain, no sinner, no sick person, no one low or despised or ill-disposed.

May the monasteries be well designed for reading and for study ; may the Order ever be in concord and may its affairs prosper.

May the monks find solitude, and seek instruction ; may they meditate without thinking of karma, avoiding all distraction.

May the nuns receive their alms and be free from quarrels and weariness ; likewise may all that have left the world be of unblemished morals.

May the wicked be startled into thought, and ever find their pleasure in destroying sin ; may they win a good destiny and therein preserve their vows unimpaired.

May the learned be well treated and gain their living from alms, with a pure lineage (of pupils), and be famed and lauded in all directions.

May beings not suffer pain in states of woe, may they be without evil actions, and with a divine body win Buddhahood.

May all Buddhas be worshipped by all beings in many ways ; may they be made wholly happy with the inconceivable bliss of Buddhas.

May the desires of Bodhisattvas for the weal of the world be accomplished ; and may all that these leaders intend for creatures be realized.

May private Buddhas be happy and likewise disciples, ever worshipped reverently by gods, asuras, and men.

May I go forth to acquiring the knowledge of my former existences and ever retain it, until I reach the Joyful stage through the help of Manjughosha.

In whatever state of life I may live, may I having strength obtain the fulness of dwelling in solitude in all my existences.

When I desire to see or to ask anything may I behold that leader Manjunatha uninterruptedly.

As the career of Manjuśrī is to accomplish the weal of all beings within the bounds of the firmament in the ten directions, even so may be my career.

As long as abides the region of space, as long as the world abides, so long may be my abiding to destroy the pains of the world.

Whatever pain there is in the world, may it all ripen in me ; and may the world be made happy by the merits of all the Bodhisattvas.

The Doctrine, the one medicine for the pains of the world, the maker of all weal and happiness, endowed with gain and honour, may it long abide.

Manjughosha I reverence, through whose favour thought is turned to good ; the good friend I salute ; prosper ye through his favour.

Bodhicaryāvatāra, x.